A History of Connecticut's Golden Hill Paugussett Tribe

A History of Connecticut's Golden Hill Paugussett Tribe

Charles Brilvitch

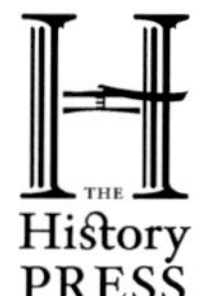

Published by The History Press
Charleston, SC 29403
www.historypress.net

All photos courtesy of the author unless otherwise stated.

First published 2007

Manufactured in the United States

ISBN 978.1.59629.296.3

Library of Congress Cataloging-in-Publication Data

Brilvitch, Charles W.
The keepers : a history of Connecticut's Golden Hill Paugussetts / Charles Brilvitch.
p. cm.
Includes bibliographical references.
ISBN-13: 978-1-59629-296-3 (alk. paper)
1. Paugusset Indians--History. 2. Paugusset Indians--Ethnic identity. 3. Paugusset Indians--Government relations. 4. Connecticut--Race relations. 5. Connecticut--Social conditions. I. Title.
E99.P292B75 2007
305.8009746--dc22
2007026830

To Chieftess Rising Star and Mary Freeman,
whose spirits would not let me rest until I got it right.

Contents

Acknowledgements 9
Introduction 11

1. From Time Immemorial 13
2. "Melting Away Before the White Man" 19
3. The Region in the Post-Revolutionary Period 23
4. Ethiope—the Tribe Regathers 27
5. Other Developments of the 1830s 37
6. Further Development at Ethiope 41
7. Ethiope Becomes Liberia 45
8. The Golden Hill Indians at Trumbull 55
9. The James Farm Community 59
10. The Dissipation of Liberia 65
11. William Sherman and the Land Base 73
12. William Sherman's Aftermath 77
13. Filling in the Blanks—Tribal Leadership and Continuity 81
14. Tribal Administration—the Twentieth Century 95
15. Conclusion 107

Appendix A 111
Notes
117
Bibliography 125

Acknowledgements

I am indebted to many people and organizations for the help they have given while my research was in progress. First, I would like to thank Chief Quiet Hawk of the Golden Hill Paugussett tribe. At no time did he give me any other directive than "Find out the truth." He graciously allowed me free use of important original documents, including William Sherman's nineteenth-century journal and the Sherman family Bible. I must also thank Kelley Wheeler of the chief's staff, who patiently walked me through countless technical difficulties and was always able to put her hands on needed materials that had sometimes been buried in file cabinets for decades.

Mary Witkowski and her staff at the Historical Collections of the Bridgeport Public Library manage one of the finest research facilities I have ever had the privilege to use. Likewise, the Trumbull Historical Society allowed me access to their entire collection and graciously permitted the use of valuable historic photographs.

I would like to express my gratitude to the late Mary McDuffie, historian of Walters Memorial A.M.E. Zion Church in Bridgeport, whose encyclopedic knowledge of long-ago events gave me a framework on which to reconstruct the tribe's "lost" history. Maisa Tisdale provided me with old family documents that, when analyzed, told much about the survival of the Native American community into the twentieth century.

Vicki Welch, the finest Native American genealogist I have ever come across, made important connections that made me realize the enormity of tribal interaction that occurred during a period when prior research efforts found nothing. She and I share the knowledge that we have barely begun to scratch the surface. And Bob Rafford made significant contributions to my understanding of the tribal community in the Naugatuck Valley and the "tentacles" of interaction that extended to the north and south.

Lastly, I need to express my gratitude to Charlie Aspinwall, ardent Paugussett supporter. Charlie works for the tribe twenty-four hours a day and was always available to help in any way possible and to proffer his special brand of dogged encouragement to the project. Without his efforts, this book never would have been brought to fruition.

Introduction

It was the perpetual Paugussett dilemma. A large and important tribe of Native Americans, the Paugussetts were on the losing side of nearly every encounter with English settlers. The tribe dwindled away over two centuries, were swindled out of all their reservation lands and disappeared practically altogether at some point between 1802 and 1823. And then Orcutt's *History of Stratford and Bridgeport* was published in 1886 containing a biography of a man named William Sherman, calling him the "last" of the Paugussett Indians (the pronouncement was quite premature, of course, as the man had children). Where *did* William Sherman come from, and just what exactly were his connections with the earlier tribal antecedents?

This question had puzzled historians for much of the twentieth century, particularly since the tribe began its quest for federal recognition in 1982. At the core of the Bureau of Indian Affairs burden of proof is a requirement that applicants demonstrate that they existed as a tribe throughout the centuries with no lapses and that they retained an intact community with both cultural and social interaction—all documented by records kept by "disinterested third-party sources." Where was any evidence of a political and social structure during those intervening years, and what had become of those "lost" members dismissed by nineteenth-century historians as having "melted away" before the advance of "white civilization?"

These were the issues that remained unresolved as I accepted a position as researcher for the Golden Hill Paugussetts in 2003. I had known two of William Sherman's descendants, Chief Quiet Hawk and his father, Chief Big Eagle, for many years. No one who has had interaction with these gentlemen could have any doubt that they absolutely know who they are and that their identity is steadfastly Native American. But how to prove it—and to a government who had conspired during that very same time period to break up tribes and assimilate their membership or move them far from their homes out to the dreaded Indian Territory—was the issue.

At the time I accepted the new position, I had been serving as historian of the city of Bridgeport since 1990 and had experienced many historical puzzles. Five years previous I had done research for the nomination of the Mary and Eliza Freeman

Houses to the National Register of Historic Places. Located on Main Street in the city's South End, they were built for "colored" women from Derby in the year 1848 in a small community peopled by other "colored" residents (in my ignorance I interpreted "colored" as African American, and to be politically correct, changed it accordingly). The long-vanished village of Ethiope, of which they were a part, had included two churches, a school, hotel, lending library, a Masonic lodge and other institutions.

Mary and Eliza Freeman had a brother by the name of Joel who was one of the founders of Ethiope and who had preceded them from Derby two decades before their arrival. Joel Freeman was obviously a man of import in the community: He was frequently executor of the estates of deceased community members and usually one of two legal witnesses present at the marriages of Ethiope residents. He was one of the three founding trustees of Zion Church, and was able to sign his name rather than use an X-mark (which may explain a good deal of his value to the community). Perhaps the most significant example of the man's political savvy and leadership is his 1841 petition to the Connecticut General Assembly requesting funds to establish a school for the village's children. It was personally satisfying for me to bring this information to light and to "resurrect" an important part of Bridgeport history that had been ignored by all previous historians.

My first few days with the Paugussett tribe, I set about to read through thousands of pages of documents in order to familiarize myself with the product of decades of prior research. Page after photocopied page of tribal overseers' reports, church baptism records, deeds, petitions for redress and other pieces of an indecipherable puzzle were crowded into binders that took up scores of storage boxes. I began to despair that anyone would ever be capable of making sense of what had taken place, much less be able to account for the "lost years."

But then I laid eyes on a deed for the sale of land owned by the survivors of the Turkey Hill Indians. Among the seven signatories was a name I recognized, and perhaps the biggest smile of my entire life lit my face as I realized the implications of its inclusion. I looked over at my office colleague and, practically laughing out loud, exclaimed, "I know who Joel Freeman is!"

I managed to keep my excitement in abeyance until I was able to check U.S. Federal Census Records. If his name had been George or Samuel or a score of others it would have been problematic, but there was in fact only one man by the name of Joel Freeman living in all of Connecticut during those years—in Derby in early life and later years in Bridgeport.

This miniscule thread of information showed me where to look. Within a short period of time it became obvious that a demonstrable Paugussett tribal member was leading a community comprised substantially of his tribesmen, building a solid and viable society whose history could be traced entirely through the public record.

It is remarkable that the Golden Hill Paugussetts came together in an urban setting and endeavored to improve their individual lives by actively participating in nineteenth-century society while preserving their tribal traditions. Following is their extraordinary story.

1.

From Time Immemorial

The Paugussett nation occupied a sizable portion of western Connecticut, generally defined as that section of coast between West Haven and Norwalk and inland up the valleys of the Housatonic and Naugatuck Rivers as far as they were navigable by canoe. The tribe was divided into four main bands, all closely related through frequent intermarriage and communal activities: the Pequannock, who occupied what is now Bridgeport, Fairfield, Stratford and Westport, with adjoining inland areas; the "Paugussett Proper," who resided mainly in Milford, Derby and Shelton; the Pootatuck, who occupied Woodbury, Southbury and Newtown; and the Weantinock, whose main village was at New Milford.

The Paugussetts were an agricultural people, and their main settlements were located where the land was flat, free from stone and had a high degree of fertility. They managed to clear hundreds of acres of virgin forest growth with fire and stone axes in order to plant their crops of corn, beans, squash and tobacco. They supplemented their crops with gathered fruits, hickory nuts and acorns from the woods. Their settlements almost always abutted good fishing locations that provided a ready source of protein. Captain John Smith described what must have been a similar area on the coast of Massachusetts Bay in 1614: "Here are many isles all planted with corn; groves, mulberries, savage gardens, and good harbors…The sea coast as you pass shows you all along good cornfields, and great troops of well-proportioned people."

Most inland inhabitants would make their way down to the coast for the summer months where they would enjoy the cool breezes, visit with kinsmen and feast on shellfish, drying some for winter sustenance. During the winter, many coastal residents would likewise journey inland to hunt deer and other game in sheltered valleys, away from the chill winds of Long Island Sound.

The large amount of cleared land and the huge size of the shell middens along the coast attested to the long periods of social order and a high degree of cooperation among tribal members. In Bridgeport, for example, there were two major villages: one on the east bank of the Uncoway (Rooster) River that was home to the Sachem, with adjoining planting fields that extended for two or three

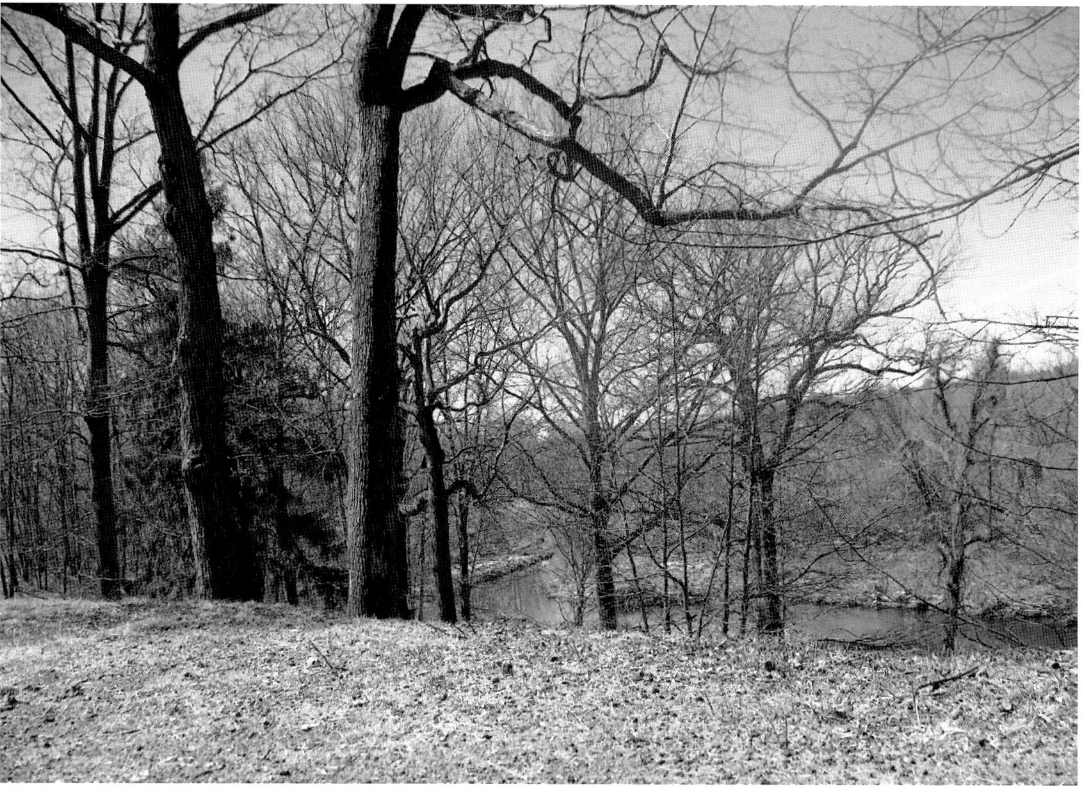

Location of the village on Uncoway (Rooster) River.

hundred acres and a fortification defended by a hundred warriors; the other at the foot of Golden Hill (today's Elm Street) with more expansive planting fields and another stronghold.

The Uncoway settlement was at a place on the river where fresh- and saltwater meet and was an ideal fishing location, especially for lamprey eel. The cleared land took up much of today's Mountain Grove Cemetery and adjacent portions of West End, and extended south to a cove at the head of Black Rock Harbor—site of the fort—opposite the corner of today's Fairfield Avenue and Orland Street.

Golden Hill was considered a sacred place due to its gushing springs (a river flowing underground from the vicinity of New Milford surfaces here). The Pequannock River on its eastern flank was ideal for weir fishing, and planting fields extended north and west from the location of the fort (west end of the present railroad bridge over the river). The village itself sat snug against the southern flank of the hill and faced a small lake that extended from Fairfield Avenue to State Street.

The Paugussetts' peaceful existence was sometimes disturbed by raids from the more warlike Pequot and Mohawk tribes, both speakers of Iroquoian languages, who exacted tribute. The Paugussetts were closely allied with their fellow Algonkian speakers—the Mahican, Wappinger and other tribes of the Hudson River Valley to the west, and

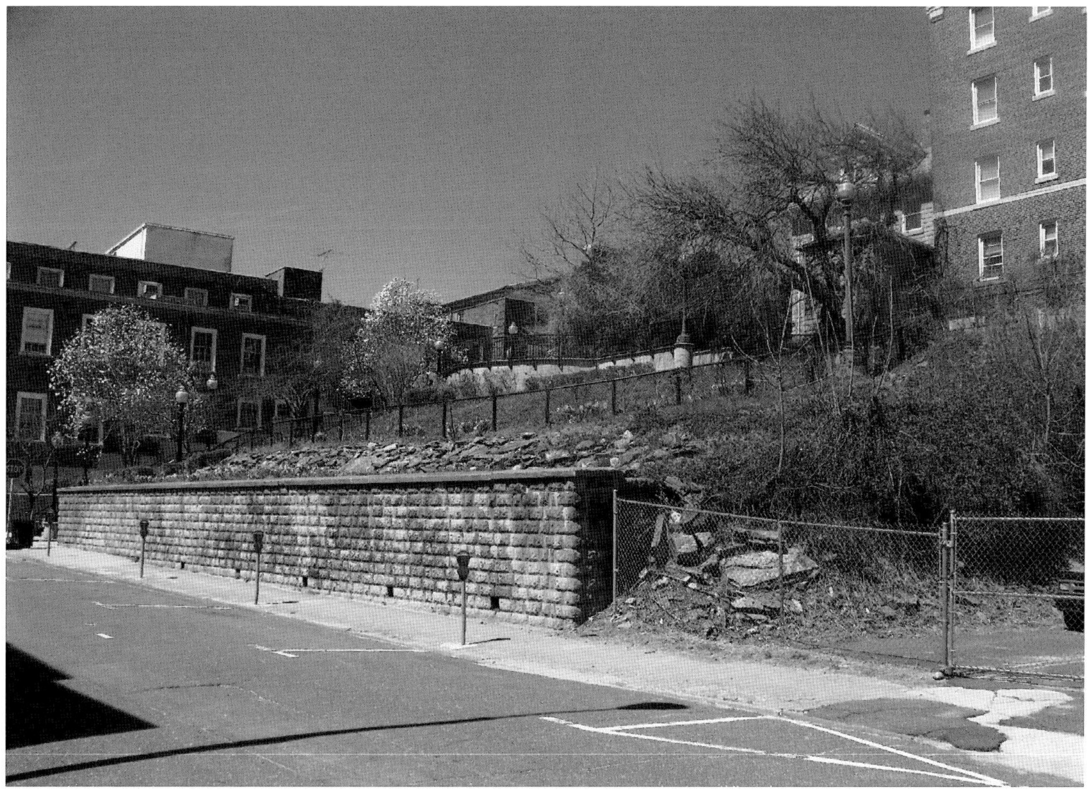

Site of the Indian village at the foot of Golden Hill.

the Shinnecock on Long Island to the south—alliances that would have reverberations centuries later.

John Cabot's "voyage of discovery" in 1497 precipitated the downfall of this Native American Eden, "claiming" the lands he found for England. Beginning with Verrazano in 1524, Europeans began to penetrate the northeast coast, frequently capturing Indians to be displayed in European cities as curiosities and later selling them off into slavery. We do have record of a few specific horrors that demonstrate the contempt with which early adventurers held the native population: A certain Captain Thomas Hunt, trading in Massachusetts Bay in 1611, was honored at a feast given by friendly Patuxet Indians. He reciprocated by inviting twenty-seven of their leaders aboard his trading ship, where they were promptly clamped in irons, shoved below deck and taken to Málaga in Spain. Here he sold them into slavery for twenty pounds sterling each.

A few years later another Englishman spent a profitable summer trading furs with the natives at Narragansett Bay. As he was readying to set sail for home, he invited the assembled tribesmen aboard his ship for a farewell party. When they had all clambered aboard, the captain and his crew opened fire with mortars and small cannon, massacring scores before they even realized what was happening.

The Dutch established a permanent foothold on the Hudson River in 1613, seriously upending the pattern of life that had existed for the Paugussetts for centuries.

Wampum—beads assembled from white and dark purple or black pieces of whelk and quahog shells respectively, which were plentiful in Long Island Sound—were often woven into belts and employed for ceremonial and diplomatic purposes by the Native Americans of the area. When the Dutch fur traders arrived, they were given a new use as currency. Suddenly this virtual monopoly of the Paugussett, the Siwanoy (who lived between Norwalk and the Bronx) and the Metoac (Long Island) was in great demand, and stronger inland tribes pressed for control of the wampum trade. The gentle farmers of the fertile coastal plain became mere vassals of the newly imposed European fur trade juggernaut.

Even more ruinous events were in the offing. A series of disease epidemics for which Native Americans had no resistance decimated the native population of Connecticut, culminating in the great smallpox epidemic of 1633–35. Entire villages were wiped out, and the remaining population was far less able to defend itself against attacks by outsiders.

By the 1630s, religious dissenters in England had moved themselves en masse to establish their "New Jerusalem" in the savage wilds of far-off New England. Founding Plymouth in 1620, their numbers exploded with the Great Migration that started eight years later, and by the early 1630s the good lands surrounding Massachusetts Bay had largely been usurped for white settlements. Looking for prime agricultural land, the Puritans helped themselves to the richest part of the Connecticut River Valley (Hartford, Wethersfield and Windsor) between 1633 and 1636.

The Pequot tribe of southeastern Connecticut remained powerful and were a serious threat to the growth of settlement. By 1637, their defiance had become intolerable, and the young colonial government launched a war to extirpate this most warlike of all Connecticut tribes. Joined by soldiers from Massachusetts, Connecticut's forces surprised the tribe in a pre-dawn raid at their main settlement. They began setting fire to the wigwams and shooting people as they attempted to flee the stockade. Between five hundred and seven hundred Pequots were slaughtered in a short period of time, and the power of the tribe was broken.

A small band did manage to escape, and they made their way westward in an effort to join up with their Iroquoian kinsmen up the Hudson River. They managed to reach as far as present-day Southport, where they were overtaken by the English. They made their last stand from a natural fortress, an island surrounded by a dense swamp, and forced the peaceable members of the local Paugussett band to stand with them (the Paugussetts were anything but friends or allies, having long been forced to pay tribute to the Pequot to prevent incursions of their warring parties).

The exhausted Indians' arrows were no match for the firearms of the militiamen, and the Great Swamp Fight ended in a complete rout of the Pequots. To ensure against any possibility that they would one day regroup and to defray the expenditures of the war effort, the governments of Connecticut and Massachusetts Bay sold some two hundred Pequot and Paugussett women and children into lifetimes of slavery.

The Puritans lost little time in capitalizing on their victory by expanding their holdings. Although the Dutch had claimed the shores of Long Island Sound as far east as the Connecticut River, the English brazenly founded the colony of New Haven at the head of a fine harbor in 1638. Encountering no immediate challenge, settlers of New Haven launched new settlements at Guilford and Milford the following year, just as the Connecticut Colony was establishing new outposts at Fairfield and Stratford. The great heartland of the Paugussett nation—location of its most important villages, shellfish reserves, burial grounds and agricultural lands—had been invaded by a people bent on securing the tribe's eventual elimination.

2.

"Melting Away Before the White Man"

We know little about what the first white settlers encountered when they came to the Paugussett lands in that year of 1639. We have no descriptions of the villages, the way of life or of prominent tribal members as we have from Jamestown and Plymouth. We only have a few terse items in the records of the Connecticut General Court. Nineteenth-century historians stitched together a plausible, if somewhat scanty, story, which included a few recorded deeds, court testimony and a good deal of conjecture, usually tempered with a fair degree of overt racism. Archeologists found evidence of village locations and summer campgrounds in virtually every likely location along the coast, giving credence to localities noted in early deeds with names such as "Wigwam Meadow" and "Old Fort."

What exactly took place in that pivotal year of 1639, and what transpired that caused this peaceful tribe of farmers and shellfish gatherers to be divested of 99 percent of their territory within a few short years? Again, we really do not know, and much that has been written is pure speculation.

What is known is that plantations were commissioned by the General Assembly at Hartford to be established at Cupheag (Stratford) and Pequonnock (Bridgeport). Roger Ludlow, then deputy governor of the Connecticut Colony and spearhead of the Pequonnock settlement effort, for some reason disobeyed the assembly's orders and proceeded to establish his town instead at Uncoway (Fairfield). He was issued a stern reprimand in October of that year. It is perhaps not unreasonable to suppose that the English planters preferred to avoid immediate conflict with the large native population centered at Pequonnock and to concentrate their efforts, at least at first, in peripheral areas that had been sparsely peopled.

There are deeds in Milford that go back to the very beginnings of the English community and trace the dealings between the leadership of the settlers and Chief Ansantawae and his subordinates. However, in the towns of Stratford and Fairfield there are no extant deeds prior to the late 1650s, and these are either for relatively minor scraps of land near the coast or for territory far back in the hinterlands.

The first volumes of both towns' land records appear to have been conveniently lost at the time the Connecticut General Court was called upon to adjudicate a settlement of the official boundary between the two towns in 1659. There may have been overlapping or conflicting titles based on treaties with the natives, or there may have been outright fraudulent seizures of land. It almost seems as though an agreement was arrived at to keep a lid on any improprieties by erasing the books and claiming that all native lands had been "conquered" as a result of the Pequot War.

The settlement of the border dispute legalized the existence of a reservation at Golden Hill, to be administered by Stratford, and two others, one at the Great Planting Field and the other at the traditional summer gathering place at Wolf Pit Neck (now within Seaside Park), both overseen by Fairfield. It was recorded that the Golden Hill tract alone held one hundred wigwams, each probably housing one or two families. Its eighty acres of rocky ground was surely insufficient to grow food to sustain a population of this magnitude.

Meanwhile, the Paugussetts received another lesson in the capabilities of their new white overlords during the Dutch war against their neighboring tribes that lasted from 1642 to 1645. Governor Kieft of New Netherlands offered the colony of Connecticut 25,000 guilders for a force of 150 men to help quell the uprising. Led by Captain John Underhill, legendary "scourge of the Indians," the Connecticut force staged a night attack on the Siwanoy fort at Greenwich, where another 500 to 700 natives were tortured and mutilated before being brutally killed. The lesson was clear: submit or face extermination.

Certainly the noose was tightening around the collective neck of the Paugussett tribe. In the aftermath of King Philip's War (1675–76), Fairfield demanded possession of the Great Planting Field, and the inhabitants of the ancient village under the bluffs along the Rooster River were abruptly divested of their hard-wrested possession. Four years later the Wolf Pit Neck land, where later generations would find hundreds of human burials, was likewise ceded to Fairfield, and all the town's natives were officially without a home. The victory of the English had been complete.

On the Stratford side of the line (demarcated by today's Park Avenue) the natives remained a viable but diminishing community, with twenty-five wigwams counted in 1710. The land (approximately bounded by today's Harrison Street, Harral and Fairfield Avenues and the Pequonnock River) included a good location for fishing weirs and a few acres of tillable ground on what was known as Indian Island (the westerly end of today's East Washington Avenue Bridge). But white farmers were carving farms out of the surrounding territory, and they habitually let their cattle and hogs pasture in the open woods, all too often finding their way to the native's unfenced cornfields. Starvation would ensue for the reservation families while the farmers' livestock grew plump for their own tables.

The Paugussett of Golden Hill lay low for decades as the world they knew intimately for millennia was turned upside down. One after another they disappeared from the reservation, in all likelihood gone to seek a more hopeful life with kinsmen in inland areas where they could still hunt and fish without restriction and hopefully eke out an

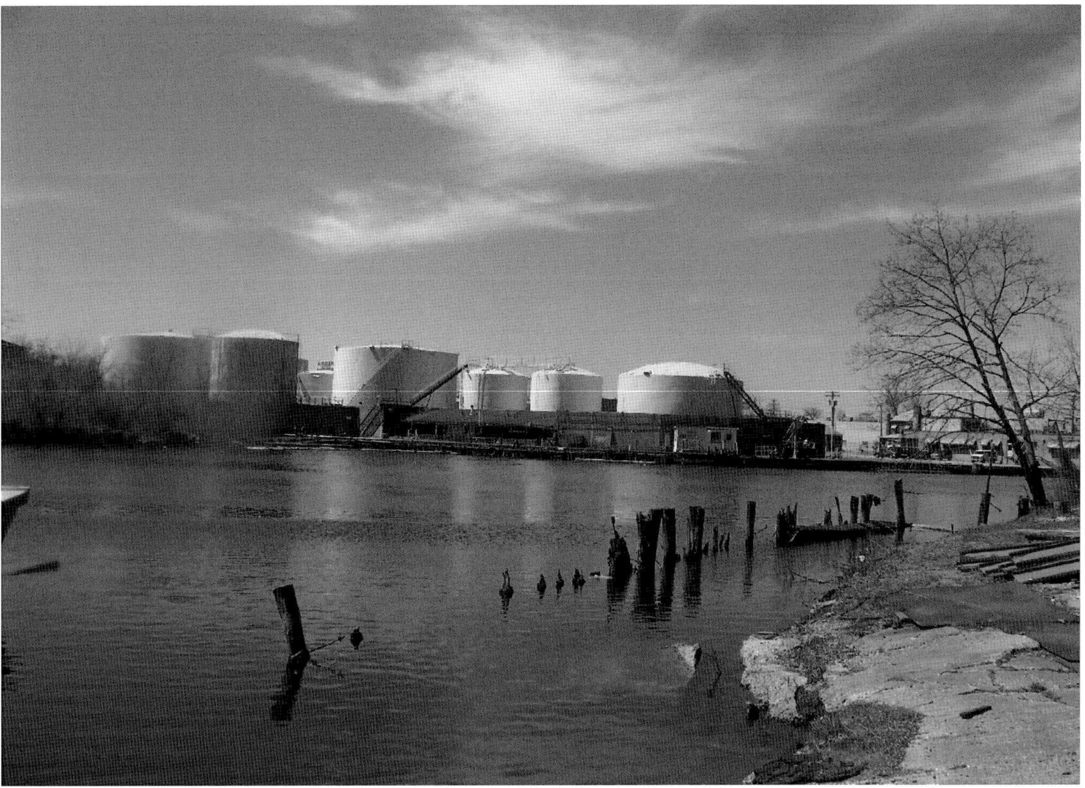

Indian Island is today the site of a tank farm on the Pequonnock.

existence. In 1763, the surviving seven Golden Hill Reservation inhabitants petitioned the General Court, complaining that twelve white inhabitants of the towns of Fairfield and Stratford had entered the reservation, pulled down the wigwams and ejected the rightful owners. The court dragged its heels before rendering a verdict two years later that said, in essence, "that's the way the cookie crumbles." They permitted those who had encroached upon the tribal lands to retain possession of sixty-eight of the eighty acres and compensated the tribe with a few blankets and barely enough corn to make it through the winter.

Following the Revolutionary War the seaport town of Bridgeport sprang into existence, and suddenly deep-water frontage on its wide river estuary became a valuable commodity. Accordingly, the tribal overseer ordered the remaining twelve acres on the Pequonnock sold in 1802 for a goodly sum (much of it going to satisfy fees that he himself had accrued). The tribal survivors were all descendants of a seventeenth-century Indian named Shoron and had by this time taken as a surname the anglicized version of his name—"Sherman." In explaining their intense devotion to the sacred place of their ancestors, Chief Quiet Hawk explained that they were "the keepers."

The story of the Milford/Stratford component of the tribe is much the same. Displaced early on from their coastal haunts, they were left with small reservations at

Turkey Hill (the Derby-Orange town line on the Housatonic River) and Corum (across the river in Shelton) in 1680. Corum was an uninhabitable rock pile, ceded back to the whites with hardly a murmur, but Turkey Hill sustained a dwindling number of Paugussett for many years. The last of it was not given up until 1826, sold "for their own benefit."

But this was certainly not the whole story. Native families who disappeared from tribal rolls, those who "scattered to the four winds" in the words of nineteenth-century historians, continued to inhabit the rural areas of western Connecticut and adjoining portions of New York State. They seldom owned property and worked for the most part as farm laborers, the occupation of much of the state's population, as virtual outcasts on the fringes of white society. They gradually adopted English surnames and the Christian faith. It is apparent from the scanty records that remain from this period (i.e. marriage certificates) that they certainly remained conscious of Paugussett identity and of one another's existence. It is as an outgrowth of this network that the nineteenth-century story of the Paugussett tribe would unfold.

3.

The Region in the Post-Revolutionary Period

1783–1815

The independence of the United States brought drastic changes to western Connecticut. The old economy based on subsistence-level agriculture and small-scale trading with the port of Boston changed almost overnight to a market economy centered on New York and other major trade links with the islands of the West Indies, Europe, South America and China. Lumbering and shipbuilding became major activities, seaports began to develop, and interconnecting roadways were laid out.

The agricultural sector prospered for a time as farmers took advantage of new markets and increased production. Rudimentary farmhouses were replaced with commodious dwellings, and village centers saw the construction of churches, schools and business structures. Many of the region's townships reached peaks of population in the period 1790–1800 that would not be seen again until the suburbanization of the latter part of the twentieth century.

As noted earlier, Fairfield and Stratford had developed in the pre-Revolutionary period as agricultural towns, and the port facilities that developed (such as the ones at Mill River, Ash Creek and two locations on the Housatonic River) were generally small wharves with a single storehouse whose proprietor supplied the nearby countryside with a few commodities such as sugar, salt, tea and rum. The major harbor lying at Bridgeport, meanwhile, lay almost wholly undeveloped until after the war's end.

Then, as if a signal had been given, development commenced in a big way. Almost all Bridgeport's present downtown streets were laid out by 1795, and wharves soon lined the head of the harbor along the Pequonnock River and the promontory known as New Pasture Point. Turnpikes were laid out by private companies leading to inland centers like Newtown, New Stratford (Monroe) and Huntington. And young men of enterprise from rural areas gravitated to the new town to take part in its economic ascendancy.

In this new circumstance, the continued existence of a reservation inhabited by rude Indians adjacent to the center of such commerce became untenable. Accordingly, the twelve remaining acres of the Golden Hill Reservation were sold off December 19,

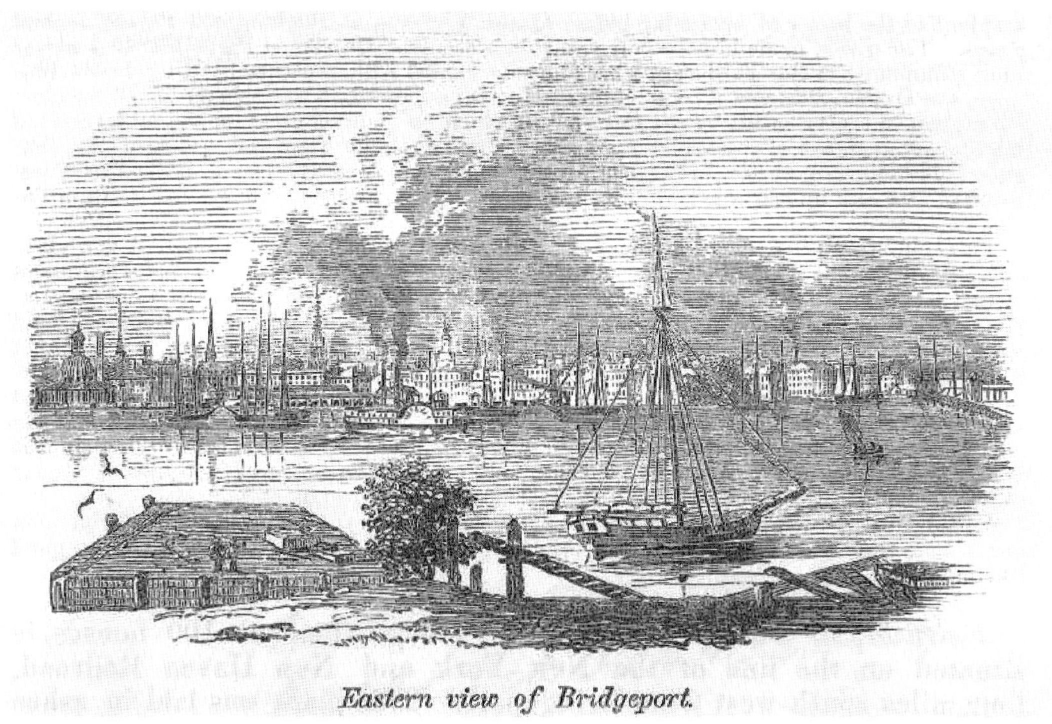

Bridgeport in its heyday as a New England seaport.

1802, for the tidy sum of $1,576, and Indian Island and the great spring of the Nimrod Lot gave way almost immediately to urban development.

Derby, too, came to prominence during this period. Located ten miles inland at the head of navigation on the Housatonic River, it had developed in its first century as an unprepossessing farm town on the east bank of the Naugatuck tributary, with its agriculture centered on the rich meadows between that river's two alternate courses. In 1784, Leman Stone (a later Turkey Hill Indian overseer) constructed a sizable storehouse and wharf where the Naugatuck and Housatonic joined. Almost immediately, development of a port town called New Boston (perhaps an indication of the progenitors' aspirations for the locality) began on adjoining land. Derby, which was ten miles closer to inland farmers than coastal locations, enjoyed a brief period of glory as one of New England's leading ports. A new bank was chartered, and the townspeople speculated heavily in the Grand Banks cod fishery in addition to trading with the islands of the West Indies.

Also in the year 1802, the reservation at Chusetown, located at the falls of the Naugatuck in what was then the upper part of Derby, was taken from the Paugussett tribe. Of value to the natives as an unrivalled fishing place, it became of importance to the whites for its water power. The land was turned over to David Humphries, who constructed a mill for the processing of wool from merino sheep, a breed he had introduced to the United States following his term as ambassador to Spain.

As with all such boom periods in early American history, this one ended abruptly, on this occasion with the Embargo Act of 1807 and the ensuing War of 1812. Derby's town fathers built a turnpike to New Haven, implausible as it may seem in retrospect, in the hope of attracting that port city's shipping commerce. Instead, the opposite occurred, followed in short order by a collapse of codfish investments and the closing of New England ports. Stratford and Milford built a bridge downstream, further impeding access to the river. New Boston was never to recover.

In the state's rural precincts there were difficult times as well. The wheat farmers of the western uplands were beset by new plant diseases and many opted to pull up stakes and move to the promising Genesee Valley in New York State. The rich lands of Connecticut's Western Reserve in northeast Ohio also opened up and beckoned multitudes of the state's young agriculturists. The population drain was underway.

1815–1830

With the curtailment of its international trading business, Bridgeport turned to a manufacturing economy. It became the national center of the saddlery business and was noted for such other products as carriages and beaver top hats (one of its major downtown thoroughfares was known as Beaver Street). Philadelphia industrialists secured the water rights on the Pequonnock River in 1828 and built a major stone mill complex for the manufacture of wool carpets—which heretofore had been imported from Europe—with power from the new Bunnell's Pond. There was even talk of constructing a canal north to the Canadian border, and Bridgeport investors bought up water rights on the Housatonic River in the towns of Kent and Cornwall, thought to have the potential to be another Lowell. While Derby languished, Bridgeport nearly doubled its population with each census and was soon to obtain a charter as a city, the first since the state's original five cities (Hartford, New Haven, New London, Norwich and Middletown) were incorporated in 1783. It is in this context that the story of the Golden Hill Paugussett tribe continues.

4.

Ethiope—the Tribe Regathers

Bridgeport became a town independent of Stratford on June 11, 1821. Census records from 1810 (when Bridgeport borough is listed separately from Stratford with a population of 572) and 1820 (when Bridgeport is undifferentiated under the Stratford heading) show a handful of "free persons of color" with surnames (e.g. Hawley, Phillips, Mitchell, Edwards) common to later generations of known Paugussetts. Although the locations of their domiciles have not been identified, it is probable that they lived in rural sections of the area in situations of poverty and isolation in common with their counterparts in other towns of Fairfield, Litchfield and New Haven Counties.

The term "colored" requires clarification in our day and age. In the first years of the nineteenth century, and for many years afterward, the census noted the race of individuals as "white" or "black" (or "African"), with "colored" (sometimes "mulatto") being somewhere in between. There was no separate category for Indians until 1870. And it should be noted that census takers apparently had significant leeway in assigning racial classification—one individual (William Sherman) was termed "white" in one census, "black" in another and "copper" when he signed on to crew a whaling vessel. After 1870, however, he was regularly enumerated as "Indian."

The origins of a community at first known as Ethiope can be traced back to 1820. In that year an existing house owned by John M. Bouton, one-half mile to the south of Bridgeport center "on the road running from the Episcopal Church to Wells Tongue" (today's Broad Street), was quitclaimed to Sheldon Smith (to be discussed later as of pivotal importance in the history of Derby).[1] Rather quickly, he resold the home to Seth Bouton Jones.[2] Jones, born 1798, was an entrepreneur who was reputed to have amassed a capital of $25,000 by the age of twenty-five.[3] He may have had abolitionist leanings, as the saddle factory he later owned was said to be "the arena of great theological discussions among the workmen."[4] At any rate, on April 10, 1821—two months before Bridgeport became an independent town—Seth B. Jones conveyed the house to people of color. John Feeley (1781–1862) and Jacob Freeman (?–1832) each secured "an undivided half interest in land and dwelling house and other buildings in Bridgeport,"[5] which suggests some sort of close relationship between these two families. Feeley and Freeman both appear on Bridgeport's first tax list in 1821, each assessed at three dollars. Tracy Freeman (1796–1861), Jacob's widow, subsequently married Miles Loudon. John Feeley is listed as a trustee of Bethel Church in the 1855 *City Directory*; his death notice[6] refers to him as Deacon. He and his wife Zilpha were listed as members of the new First Methodist Church in 1823,[7] as was Tracy Freeman (Jacob, however, was a member of St. John's Episcopal Church at the time of his death).

In 1825, four years after the property was sold by Jones, they were joined by Benjamin Freeman (1763–1843), who purchased his lot from Timothy Risley (1780–1856), and settled immediately to the south of Feeley and Jacob Freeman.[8] Benjamin is listed in the census at Milford in 1810, and in 1820 in the northerly part of Stratford in proximity to Marcus B. "Mark" Freeman, one of the founders of the James Farm community to be discussed later. He appears to be the brother of a Thomas Freeman, whosc surname is shown on an 1808 Stratford deed[9] "alias Edwards." Benjamin raised his family in this house, and these family members would play important roles in the community's later development.

In 1830, a third Freeman, Philip of Fairfield, built a home to the south of Benjamin. He paid $158 for the lot.[10] He appears to have run into financial difficulty, however, and in 1833 was remanded to prison. His property was seized for nonpayment of a $10.75 debt to Seth B. Jones.[11] He may have died in prison, as he makes no further appearance in the public record.

The land in this part of Bridgeport may have been considered undesirable to whites due to the proximity of salt marshlands and the threat of malaria. Also, an adjoining parcel of land had been leased by Timothy Risley for use as a lampblack factory[12] and later a turpentine works,[13] neither particularly desirable adjuncts to quality residential districts. Rufus Shepard (originally of Newtown) described these premises in a deed dated August 14, 1832:[14]

> *A certain parcel of buildings consisting of a lampblack kiln and a wood building adjoining for the storage of and use of lampblack, etc. Situated on land of Timothy Risley and wife near Wells Tongue in Bridgeport leased to Nehemiah Robbins for turpentine factory with an agreement to said Robbins to lease a privilege on the same for the above mentioned property for the same term of time of his own lease with privileges to & from etc.*

In 1829, Benjamin Freeman's daughter Rosanna (named an heir in an 1851 deed)[15] and her husband John Johnson, likely an African American born circa 1800 in Maryland,[16] purchased land on what was to become Whiting Street and built a home overlooking the mouth of a salt creek (Pond Gutter) and Bridgeport's lower harbor.[17] The marriage record for their daughter in a later period[18] indicates that she had been born in Plymouth, Connecticut, in 1829, placing the family in the center of Underground Railroad activity just prior to their taking up residence in Bridgeport. John Johnson was the wealthiest man of his generation in the Ethiope community, with real estate assets valued at

$8,000 at the time of the 1850 census. He died in 1856; Rosanna died in 1864. The Johnsons' son, John Jr., was listed as pastor of Bethel A.M.E. Church in the 1857–58 *City Directory*.

The land east of the Johnsons' was sold to a man named Joel Freeman who had reportedly come to Bridgeport in 1828 from Derby[19] and who worked as a sailor on a West India schooner. He purchased an old shop building from Rufus Shepard,[20] and on September 21, 1831, he purchased a harbor-front lot[21] located 247 feet east of Main Street, the only deep-water frontage in the community. It would be used in later years as a site for baptisms.[22]

Joel Freeman was the linchpin in the founding of the Ethiope community. He was irrefutably a Turkey Hill Paugussett—as one of the heirs of John Howd, Turkey Hill chieftain, he was a petitioner for the sale of tribal land at Beaver Hill in 1840.[23] He was also a founding trustee of Zion Church and a petitioner to the Connecticut General Assembly for funds to organize a school for "colored children." He served in positions of trust throughout his years in Bridgeport, including serving as executor of the estates of deceased Ethiope residents.

Joel was the eldest son of Timothy (1761–1841) and Sebina Freeman (1766–1843) who are listed in census records through 1820 (and also in 1843–44 Derby Land Records)[24] under the surname Hull. They owned property in a part of Derby known as Deerfield totaling twelve acres and known as the "rock house lot,"[25] which was immediately adjacent to Eunice Mack (a known Golden Hill Paugussett) and Jeremiah Merrick (a known Turkey Hill Paugussett). Jeremiah was in fact married to a Sylvia Freeman and had a daughter who was named Eliza Freeman, likely indicating a close familial relationship.

One hundred years after the organization of Zion Church, an article in the April 1, 1928 *Bridgeport Sunday Post* recounts the story of its organization:

> *A band of Negroes* [an incorrect assumption on the part of the newspaper correspondent] *inhabiting the farms and woods around the embryo town of Bridgeport met one summer evening under the shadow of a great elm tree that stood where the public library is now located. This huge tree constituted a sort of open air forum for the Negroes who were wont to meet under its spreading branches, hold divine service, and discuss the general situation.*

It was a notable event locally when this tree was cut down on February 6, 1873. Joel Freeman's role in this meeting cannot be ascertained from a distance of eighteen decades, although it does happen to coincide neatly with his arrival in Bridgeport. What is known is that he is named first among three trustees of the church when a lot was purchased[26] and, perhaps significantly, was able to sign his name rather than use an X-mark. Immediately upon the repayment of the church note on March 11, 1843,[27] Joel Freeman was able to purchase land adjoining his homestead,[28] almost certainly indicating that he had put up his own unsecured funds for construction of the church that were repaid at that time.

The community began to coalesce remarkably after 1830. It may be no coincidence that this was the year that President Andrew Jackson signed into law the Indian Removal Act, decreeing that Native Americans either assimilate into mainstream society or be removed to the dreaded Oklahoma Territory far beyond the Mississippi River.

The mid-1830s were an economic boom time in America, and Bridgeport was expanding with alacrity. On October 3, 1836, it was incorporated as a city, and new charter privileges enabled city fathers to bond for construction of the Housatonic Railroad. This great enterprise was to bring the trade and produce of the western part of the state—then including the bulk of American iron production—down to tidewater at Bridgeport, and to connect the city with Albany, New York. The purpose of this link was to provide a reliable route for goods coming east on the Erie Canal to an ice-free harbor during the winter months when the Hudson River was frozen over. The railroad opened in 1840 (when Bridgeport's population stood at 4,570), and, in spite of the financial Panic of 1837, it led the city to a new level of prosperity.

Ethiope prospered as well. In 1841, the residents of the community (almost exactly consistent with the enumeration of "free persons of color" in the 1840 census for Bridgeport) petitioned the Connecticut General Assembly for funds to organize a school. The list of petitioners was headed by Joel Freeman,[29] and he alone seems to have had no children who would have benefited from its creation. It reads:

> *The petition of the undersigned inhabitants of the Town of Bridgeport in Fairfield County, humbly shewith, that there are in the said Town of Bridgeport, and now belonging to the Stratfield School Society fifty-eight colored children between the ages of four and sixteen for whom Said Society is entitled to draw money from the school fund—That most of said children reside in a village, at the Southern extremity of Bridgeport, at least a mile distant from the school house in the district to which they belong; That many of them are, consequently, for a considerable part of every year, prevented by storms &ct. from traveling and attending school; That the distinction of color, and the prejudices existing in the community upon the subject, render the situation of colored children, in all district schools, and especially in the District School to which most of the children above named belong, as that district embraces within its limits the greater part of the City of Bridgeport, extremely unpleasant & disadvantageous that, owing to these causes, many of the colored children above referred to neglect attending school at all, while the Subscribers, with others have for some time endeavored to keep up a school for the whole education of colored children, but having no benefit from the public money, they have labored under great difficulties and embarrassments, and unless the Legislature grant relief, they fear that the object must be abandoned. The undersigned can not regard it as just, that the money drawn from the public fund on account of colored children should be appropriated in such a way that they can derive but little benefit from it—They therefore pray that all the inhabitants within the certain limits to be fixed by the General Assembly being wholly in said Stratfield School limits or all the colored families in said society should be constituted a school District by the name of* [-blank-] *District; & be entitled to all the privileges of other Districts in said School Society—Or that such other relief may be*

granted as may be just & proper, and the Petitioners, as in duty bound will ever pray—Dated at Bridgeport April 21st 1841.

Petitioners' names—
Joel Freeman
John Johnson
Simeon Dixon
Thomas Burton
William Allen
Nelson Judd
Alson B. Judd
Tunis Green
James Carey
John Feeley
Richard VanAlstine
Philander Pitts

The petition was successful. A committee was appointed and land was purchased for school construction on July 24, 1845.[30]

Joel Freeman went on to financial, as well as other, attainments that must have increased his stature in his community. He eventually owned a total of four houses, three of which he built himself, and the last he acquired from the estate of John Johnson in 1856.[31] Joel is listed in the first Bridgeport *City Directory* (1855) at 21 South Third (today's Whiting) Street, and his tenant, Rensselaer Pease, is listed at 19 South Third Street, directly on the harbor front. Pease was a boat builder and known Golden Hill Paugussett who worked in the ship carpentry business in partnership with Reuben Cam. Cam's first wife was a Rhoda Freeman,[32] who was likely a cousin of Joel's. Late in life, both Cam and Pease appear to have married the same woman—and to have been married to her simultaneously. In October 1850, Rensselaer Pease married Caroline Jackson of Litchfield—in Litchfield—and remained married to her until his death April 24, 1856. In October 1851, Reuben Cam also married Caroline Jackson of Litchfield—in Bridgeport. Alain C. White's *History of the Town of Litchfield 1720–1920* refers to her as "Crazy Caroline" and states, "[She] was really out her mind and used to parade the streets with corn silk curls and a small branch for a parasol."[33]

Rensselaer almost certainly resided at 19 South Third Street with his daughter, Olive(tte), who was aged seven and in his household in the 1850 census for Bridgeport. Pivotal Golden Hill Paugussett William Sherman (1825–1886) listed Bridgeport as his place of residence when he signed on the crew of a whaling ship in 1848 and also on his marriage record in 1853. It may well be that he, too, resided for a time with the man generally believed to be his father, Rensselaer Pease, at Joel Freeman's house.

Joel Freeman married twice. His first wife was Nancy Phillips (1808–1850), a daughter of Philip Moses (known Turkey Hill Paugussett) and probably his own

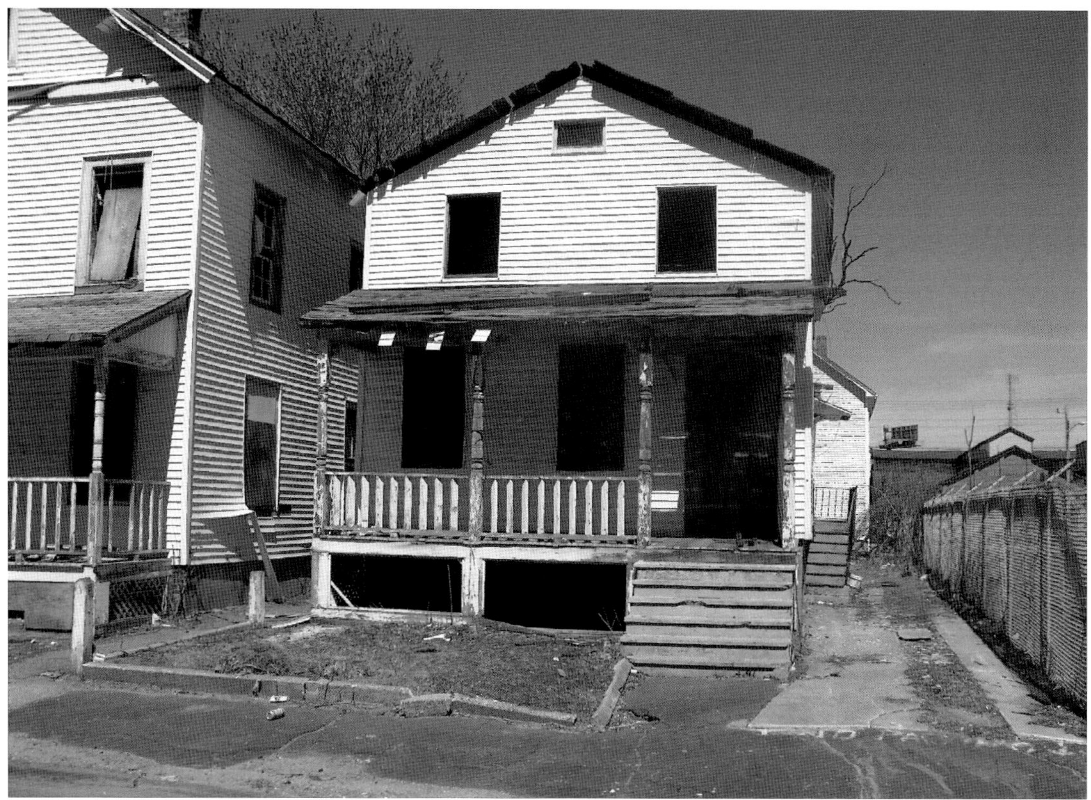

The historic school building stood abandoned and vandalized at 188 Gregory Street, four blocks from its original location at Main and Whiting Streets until its destruction by fire in July 2007.

cousin. She appears to have remained in Derby throughout her lifetime. His second wife was Chloe (born circa 1802), who was the sole other occupant of his Bridgeport household in the 1850 and 1860 census. She died in the Ethiope homestead in 1862.

Joel himself died in Bridgeport on April 29, 1865, at the age of seventy-four, just as the Civil War came to a close.[34] It is perhaps indicative of the reasons native people began to seek their fortunes in Bridgeport to compare the inventory of Joel's estate to that of his brother Amos, who had died in the rural town of Huntington some years earlier. Amos's meager possessions, including a "½ acre of land with an old house on the same," seem to reveal a hardscrabble life of privation, with a value of only $28.87. Joel's possessions were valued at nearly one hundred times that amount, including "one tract of land with four dwelling houses and other outbuildings thereon, bounded northerly by Whiting Street, easterly and southerly by creek and westerly by land, formerly owned by Rosanna Johnson, deceased" and "the undivided one half of a block of three tenements, together with the land on which they are located, and situated west and near the North African Church on Broad Street." The one lease agreement that survives from this latter property[35] indicates it was rented to Garrison Murray, a Zion Church officer.

Joel's possessions seem to reveal the life of a man of culture and material success. He certainly took advantage of his harbor-front location and its ready food source, as indicated by his "2 eel spears," "1 oyster drag," "1 flat center board boat, sail & one oar" and "2 small oars." He owned books, pictures, a map, a "portrait of a child" and "3 violins and 1 flute." The inventory shows an unusually large number of linens for a household of two people, suggesting the presence of frequent guests. The possibility exists that Freeman (and his next-door neighbor Johnson) might have been operatives of the Underground Railroad, in which other Native American tribes are known to have participated, and that Bridgeport Harbor was the point from which escaping enslaved people were conducted to the major station forty-one miles north at Plymouth. It has long been part of the Long Island Shinnecock tribe's folklore that they ferried escaping slaves across Long Island Sound to the Connecticut side.

The settlement of known Native Americans at the Ethiope community surrounding Joel Freeman's property raises another question: Could there have been a memory of the ancient summer gathering place at Wolf Pit Neck, which adjoined Ethiope? A period of 150 years had passed between the time of its cession to the English and the date of Joel Freeman's initial lot purchase. It is known that this site included an expansive burial ground.[36] A passage in Orcutt's *History of the Old Town of Derby*[37] may offer insight into the length of the collective Native American recollection:

> *In the spring of 1831 a company of Indians, consisting of about thirty men, women, and children, from the shores of Lake Champlain, came to the point (Milford) and encamped for a number of days, perhaps fifteen. They were led by an old patriarch or a chieftain of "eighty winters," whom they appeared to obey and reverence. They conversed in the Indian tongue, and some of them knew but little English. They had a tradition that some of their ancestors lived at Pocomoc Point, and said that they had come for the last time to the hunting ground of their fathers. These were no doubt descendants of the Paugasuck tribe, whose ancestors had removed from Milford to Turkey Hill, Paugassett, Pootatuck or Newtown, and who went back yearly to Milford to catch and dry oysters, spending the summer at a watering place.*

The *Bulletin of the Archeological Society of Connecticut* contains an article titled "Indian Archeology in and around Bridgeport, Connecticut" by C.S. Batchelor and R. Edward Steck. In this article, they identify Welles' Tongue, location of Ethiope, as the site of a pre-contact native village, with a shell heap "at the site of the old Locomobile Plant" (earlier the lampblack/turpentine works) and numerous burials found when the Seaside Park seawall was being constructed.[38] They made note of a "stone axe of tremendous size weighing fourteen pounds...found at the foot of Henry Street"—the opposite side of Pond Gutter from Joel Freeman's homestead.

The Freeman Family Compound Expands and Diversifies

With the Ethiope village starting to take shape, speculative builders moved in and began the process of extending the village by selling constructed homes to probable

Native Americans. Between 1831 and 1835, the west side of Main Street north of Whiting was built up, and new families arrived to purchase and occupy the houses.

In the earliest instance of such an exchange, David Curtis sold a building lot to Elias Hodge (1799–1867) who, in common with all the Ethiope builders of whom we have knowledge, was white. This occurred on December 2, 1831,[39] and the price paid was $108.50. On October 5, 1833, Hodge conveyed the property "with buildings thereon standing" to Henry Cooke for $740,[40] with a mortgage of $440.[41] Cooke had arrived from "Putnam, New York,"[42] the county lying between Danbury, Connecticut, and the Hudson River that was home to the Mahican tribe. By the time the 1855 *City Directory* was published, the property included a grocery run by Reverend Leonard Collins, pastor of Zion Church. Henry Cooke died sometime between 1844 and 1846 and the property passed to his wife, Presence, who was by 1850 known as Presence Jackson (she may have followed native tradition and reverted to her maiden name as there is no record of a marriage and at no time is there a discernable man in her household with the name Jackson).

Presence Jackson (born circa 1800) was a woman of import in the community. She is listed in the 1850 census in the home of showman P.T. Barnum, Iranistan, which was about one mile from Ethiope, where she quite possibly worked as his cook. (The 1860 census indicates that she was a steamboat cook, as was her son-in-law with whom she resided. Hamilton Jackson, who married Olive Pease, is also listed as a steamboat cook in this census, although a relationship to Presence has not been established.) Presence Jackson is again mentioned in 1853 when her mortgage is released.[43] She is last listed in the Bridgeport *City Directory* for 1871 as Mrs. Presence Tate, widow of Thomas (no marriage or death records found), and was alive as late as April 1873, when she and John H. and Ellen Deming (her daughter and son-in-law) obtained a $5,200 mortgage against the property.[44] The Deming family will be discussed shortly.

Builders Oliver and William Sherman (copartners and dealers for firm of O. & W. Sherman) obtained the lot south of Henry Cooke on April 21, 1834.[45] On September 23 of that same year they conveyed it to Tunis Green "with buildings thereon standing" for $500.[46] Tunis Green (1803–1856) came to Ethiope from Redding, Connecticut, site of the Paugussett Lonetown reservation, where he was enumerated in the 1820 census and where he married Rosanna Brush of Newtown on November 28, 1822,[47] almost certainly the sister of Chloe, who was married to Agrippa Pease. His Bridgeport death record,[48] however, tells us that he had been born in "Pokeepsie [sic]," New York, as were William Sherman and other Ethiope residents, including Henry W. Morris and Sarah Vanlien.

Tunis, or Teunis, is a Dutch name, as is Rensselaer. A substantial number of Ethiope's inhabitants are listed in census records as born in New York State, and many seem to have come from the Dutchess, Putnam and Columbia County area, where late eighteenth-century Indian deeds have been found with the signature of Tom Sherman (died 1801), Golden Hill/Pootatuck Paugussett. This territory is known to have been a place of refuge for Paugussett Indians during the seventeenth and eighteenth centuries. In the 1840s, Ethiope community member Eliza Hayes (landlady in the 1870 census to the family of John Pease, son of Agrippa and known Paugussett) ran a tavern at Wall and Water Streets in the Bridgeport business district that was known as the Knickerbocker House,[49] perhaps named in deference to the former home of many of her customers.

Tunis Green's daughter Caroline had married James Purdy of Newtown on December 21, 1835,[50] and Purdy provided money to refinance his father-in-law's mortgage during hard financial times in 1842.[51] Tunis Green was also the recipient of secured loans from William P. Edwards of Trumbull and Alvira Edwards of Bridgeport.[52] When the second loan was repaid, the quitclaim deed named as grantors "James Purdy & Alvira Purdy his wife [late Alvira Edwards]." Tunis eventually achieved a measure of prosperity as well, and there were three houses on his lot by the time of his death. He left his property to his grandson George H. Purdy,[53] who is mentioned in Paugussett William Sherman's journal as a friend and co-worker.[54] A William Sherman had a claim of $13.50 against the estate, but it is not known whether this was the Golden Hill Paugussett Indian who listed Bridgeport as his home in that year of 1853 or the white builder who had sold Tunis Green his property two decades previous (both individuals were alive at the time).

To the south of Tunis Green, at the corner of Whiting Street, a third house completed the row. It was sold on September 1, 1835, to Isaac Hammond and Joseph Bloom.[55] Bloom (1812–1873), a native of Suffolk County, Long Island, home of the Shinnecock tribe,[56] had been married to Adeline Deming (sister of Presence Jackson's son-in-law) only nineteen days previous[57] (she had earlier been married to Timothy Starr, of the Monroe Paugussett family.)[58] Bloom bought out the interest of the deceased Hammond in 1843.[59] He became a man of means who was able to provide mortgage money to fellow inhabitants of Ethiope.[60] His widow Adeline remained an Ethiope resident until 1903, the last inclusion of her name appearing in the 1903 *City Directory*.

The Demings were important members of their community almost from its inception. Parents John and Rachel originally came from Woodbury, Connecticut, thirty-three miles to the north of Ethiope. John is listed in the 1820 census in Middlebury (adjoins Woodbury), and in Bridgeport in 1830, residing at that time on New Pasture Point on the east side of the Pequonnock River. A Mary Deming, who appears to have been his aunt, died unwed in the town of Southbury (also adjoining Woodbury) in 1858 at the age of eighty-three.[61] Her birthplace is given as Trumbull, which would place an earlier generation of the family in proximity to the Golden Hill Indians. There is a family recollection of Native American descent,[62] as well as memory of Presence Jackson's employment with P.T. Barnum and the fact that the family had come from "either Middletown or Middlebury."

John H. had a brother George F., a seaman, who lived on Broad Street in the house that had belonged to Benjamin Freeman.[63] He was married to Amelia Sills of Bridgeport (likely Golden Hill Paugussett) on July 9, 1848.[64] John H. and Ellen had either a boarder or servant in their home in the 1850 census named Mahala Pease—Rensselaer's daughter. The Demings were pillars of Zion Church and served it in a number of positions of import: John H. was trustee, treasurer and superintendent of the Sunday School;[65] Ellen was secretary of an affiliate organization called the Daughters of Zion.[66]

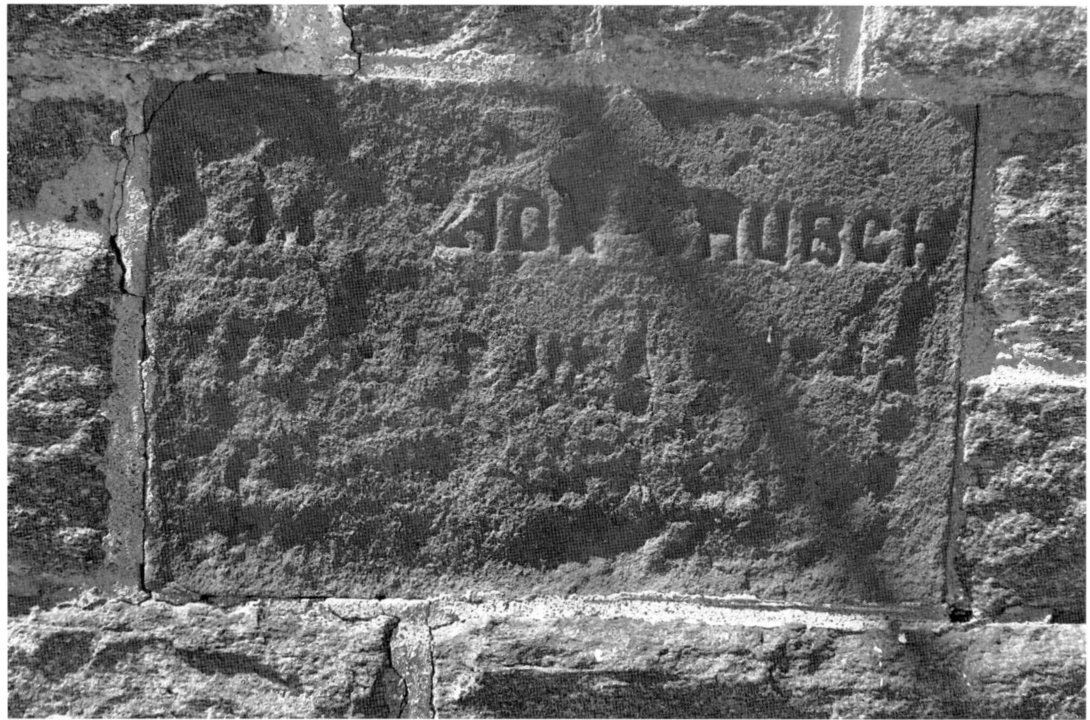

The original cornerstone of Zion Church, preserved and incorporated into the foundation of the present 1882 building.

That summer of 1835 marked a seminal milestone in the history of the fledgling community. As noted previously, Zion Colored Methodist Episcopal Church[67] purchased land on Broad Street at the head of Whiting Street on June 12 of that year (trustees, in addition to Joel Freeman, were Grant and Peter Hawley, grandsons of Nero Hawley, a slave from Trumbull who had won his freedom by fighting in the Revolution). Construction must have commenced immediately, as a local diarist, William Wheeler, noted that the cornerstone was placed on July 5. At long last, the residents of the Ethiope community, and people of color from all of western Connecticut, would have a house of worship of their own as well as a central gathering place and focal point.

5.

Other Developments of the 1830s

Derby

Derby was transformed once again during the boom years of the 1830s. A native son, Sheldon Smith, had moved to Newark following the collapse of Derby's economy and took part in that New Jersey city's first great wave of industrial development. He returned to Connecticut convinced that his moribund hometown, with its ample water power, could follow suit. He bought up the area known as Derby Neck, between the Naugatuck and Housatonic Rivers, laid out streets of building lots (named Caroline, Elizabeth, Minerva and Ophelia for his daughters) and in 1832 built a substantial canal to channel power from the Naugatuck for the factories that were soon under construction. Once again telegraphing ambitious hopes, he christened the new metropolis Birmingham.

Derby, however, did not witness the corresponding development of a community of nonwhites. The town had been the seat and the election place for the black governors of Connecticut in the eighteenth and early nineteenth centuries. Black governors, comparable to kings in royal provinces, provided leadership to people of color and enforced order in the colonies of British North America and the states of the early republic. They were elected annually by slaves and freedmen.

Perhaps Derby, with its dreams of becoming one of the nation's great industrial centers, was becoming somewhat unfriendly to its "anachronistic" African and Native American inhabitants. An early twentieth-century newspaper story derived from Orcutt and Beardsley's history of Derby recounts an incident from the period that would seem to suggest the atmosphere prevalent under the new order:

> *In 1833, a squaw came from Milford, who became the guest of James Mack. She was stricken ill and was immediately removed to Milford, where she died of smallpox. In the Deerfield settlement were Jerry Mack and four other Indian men, two squaws and three children.*
>
> *In due time these 10 Indians fell victims to the dread smallpox, and all died with the exception of the three children. These children were run down in the hills and made immune from the ravages of the disease. They were vaccinated by a Dr. Kendall.*

The Indians were buried by Dr. Samuel Bassett and others who had had the smallpox, in the garden near their huts. Derby paid all the burial expenses and great excitement prevailed in the village as to the disease, and to make sure that no more Indians should become paupers from that settlement, the torch was applied to these modern wigwams. They were reduced to ashes. This was by order of the selectmen.

Incidents such as this routing of Derby's remaining native people and the imprisonment of Philip Freeman for a minor debt almost seem to have created a resolve within the Ethiope community at this time to put an end to their collective powerlessness and to pursue material prosperity on the white man's terms—through the ownership of real estate and the establishment of viable businesses. In time, many would succeed.

Waltersville

America was rife with land speculation in the 1830s. Paper cities were created by the score, with the majority never again heard of in the aftermath of the financial Panic of 1837.

One such development was the Cottage Domain laid out on ten acres on the easterly side of the Pequonnock River, a scant mile distant from Ethiope. Its progenitor was William P. Greene of Norwich (1795–1868), partner and agent of the Thames Manufacturing Company, president of the Thames Bank and one-time mayor of his city. A plan for this development[68] shows a circular English park called Franklin Place at the center of "54 eligible building lots." William H. Noble recounted the inception of this subdivision in his treatise "East Bridgeport by Personal Observation," included in Orcutt's *History of Stratford and Bridgeport*: [69] "William P. Green...through the agency of his brother abolitionist, Mr. Jocelyn, of New Haven, made a purchase of some seventy acres belonging to Benjamin Brooks. On this he commenced the improvement that is known as Walter and Green Streets, building a few small houses. He also built a dwelling for his agent, George Walter." Bridgeport people must have identified the development with the local agent, for an 1845 deed[70] describes "property at Walterville [sic], formerly called Cottage Tract."

Waltersville was perhaps too small to support its own church and other institutions, and its inhabitants were associated with those established at Ethiope. Residents in the 1840 census included Eliza Cam (with three in her household, all female—she was to marry Edward Hawley of Newtown on June 30, 1846)[71] and "Ransler" Pease. The 1850 census showed Rensselaer Pease still in residence adjacent to Charles and Susan Jackson, whose daughter, born June 7, 1849,[72] was named Presence, a likely indication that Charles was a son of the Presence Jackson discussed previously. The 1862 Bridgeport *City Directory* lists "Harriet Pease, wid[ow] William," who had been a son of the known Paugussett Agrippa. The community remained viable for some decades: When William Sherman Jr. left his father's Trumbull home, he set up house in Waltersville at 288 Pembroke Street.[73] Sherman had married Jane Phoenix January 3, 1880,[74] daughter of Reverend

H.R. Phoenix, the Zion Church pastor. With the solitary exception of the Jacksons (and Hurd does mention a Jackson family as known Golden Hill Paugussetts),[75] all the families mentioned have confirmed ties to the Paugussett tribe.

Newfield

A third community, on the easterly flank of Bridgeport Harbor, grew out of the 1830s speculative boom. Located outside the limits of the new city in the town of Stratford (it would be annexed to Bridgeport in 1889), Newfield appears to be more the product of the real estate bust after 1837 than a deliberate attempt by a dedicated abolitionist to create decent housing for people of color.

Edwards Johnson (1804–1873) was the grandson of William Samuel Johnson, one of the framers of the United States Constitution (his great-grandfather had founded King's College, later Columbia University). Born to wealth and privilege, he and his brother William began the purchase and consolidation of much of the land in the margins of the Great Meadows salt marsh and the east shore of Bridgeport Harbor during the 1820s, diking and draining some portions—evidently intent on conducting large-scale farming operations. In 1831–33, Edwards built a twenty-eight-room manor house that he named Eagle's Nest (destroyed by arsonists in June 2006). Orcutt later noted that Sarah Sherman of the Golden Hill tribe married Ben Roberts, "Negro," and resided at Eagle's Nest. In an article describing the great house, which appeared in the *Bridgeport Standard* on August 28, 1915, Helen Harrison noted, "A small boy made his way into the attic recently to investigate the date and found...the name T.A. Roberts and the date Mar. 1848 on a beam close to the end of the house. The Robertses were a family who made gardens and did other such work for people in the neighborhood."

Johnson chose the tract of land closest to the nascent city to be "surveyed and laid out into lots by Daniel Wakelee August 24, 1836...[including] a lot of 6 acres from which the Water of the Sea is excluded by a dyke...also certain Highways or Streets and a 'Public Square' laid down on such map."[76] His advertisement entitled "Seventy Building Lots"[77] reads:

> *The subscriber offers for sale seventy valuable Building Lots, near the east line of the City and lying upon the Harbor of Bridgeport, within a few minutes walk of the center of that flourishing place, presenting every convenience to the mechanic, manufacturer or the man of leisure; the front lots lying directly upon the Boston and New York mail stage road, and the rear commanding a fine view of the harbor and city of Bridgeport, and Long Island Sound; offering by their vicinity to the City, every inducement as a residence to the man of business, and by their healthy and commanding situation, everything desirable for the most elegant country seats.*

Johnson's timing was unfortunate as the Panic of 1837 would shortly devastate the nation's economy and, being highly leveraged, he was soon on the road to financial ruin. Letters to his brother William, a lawyer who resided in New York,[78] reveal increasing financial desperation as he pleads for additional loans. On November 23, 1836, he writes, "Advertisements for my land...might chance the attraction of capitalists to it and make those in these parts think that I am in earnest." He tells of "lots sold to Dr. Middlebrooks...he intends to build a large carriage factory" (no such transaction has been located in land records). He poignantly adds, "As you know, I am the poorest dog in the land."

Johnson sold only one lot that year for $200 to a man named John Goodwin who was in foreclosure by 1840.[79] On March 26, 1839, he writes to William of the "great freshet," which swept away the milldam on the Pequonnock River and the bridge that a certain Birdseye Noble had built leading to yet another projected city on that river's east bank. Johnson wrote wistfully of "the town that was to rival mine."

Into this situation stepped Captain Henry C. Burroughs who purchased four lots on September 17, 1839, for the fire sale price of $350 in total,[80] and two more five weeks later for $150.[81] Burroughs began to turn these empty lots over in a matter of months to people of color at a price of $384 each.[82] Census records show that many heads of household in this new community had been born in Maryland and Virginia and that a majority of the men were employed as seamen. This may be explained by information contained in Captain Burroughs's obituary, which displays the extent of his involvement in maritime trade:[83] "For many years he was engaged in the West India trade, and afterward in the Boston coasting trade, at one time owning a number of vessels."

6.

Further Development at Ethiope

Waltersville and Newfield have been discussed in passing to show by contrast what Ethiope was not: a planned housing tract laid out by whites with little provision for the evolution of a truly viable community. Ethiope had no single paternalistic figure who conceived of a grand plan and went off to peddle building lots. Rather, it appears that the community's development was entirely self-engendered, with residents themselves approaching landowners, engaging builders and planning every phase of its growth to suit their own needs.

Zion Church appears to have been a catalyst for new growth in the community despite the darkening economic climate. Lawzon Sherman (1795–1842), a builder from the town of Monroe, secured a parcel of land on the south side of Whiting Street to the west of John Johnson from David Curtis on April 1, 1837. Sherman paid sixty dollars, with a mortgage for the full amount.[84] He conveyed the property back to Curtis two years later[85] "with the dwelling houses thereon standing including all the stone belonging to me on and near the premises."

The stone may have been of use to the purchaser of the first house, Alson B. Judd (1797–1864), who was listed in the 1850 census as a mason. Judd paid $300 for a house and lot adjoining John Johnson on January 28, 1841.[86] He had been married to Catherine Edwards, yet another member of that widespread Paugussett clan, on November 25, 1827.[87] His previous residence had been at Danbury.[88] Alson's brother Nelson (married to Jane Sauls of Bridgeport, another likely Paugussett, on August 10, 1846)[89] owned an interest in the house prior to his removal to Schenectady, New York.

The second house, west of Alson Judd, was conveyed to William H. Davis (1797–1894) on June 28, 1841,[90] also for the sum of $300. Davis was a seaman born in Maryland, as was his neighbor John Johnson. William Sherman's journal makes mention of his procuring clams from Davis. The name of Davis's first wife, with whom he resided in New York, is unknown. His second wife was Catherine E. Ambler of Bethel,[91] apparently a cousin of Franklin Ambler, Sherman's employer who was known for giving annual clambakes. His third wife (married October 8, 1848) was Mary Ann Allen.[92] Davis owned real estate valued at $5,000 in the 1870 census, and he is shown as a trustee of Zion Church in the 1871–72 *City Directory*. His death notice appeared in the *Bridgeport Evening Post* on March 19, 1894 (front page), in which he was referred to as "the oldest colored resident of the city." The newspaper gave his age as "97 years, 1 month, 20 days."

The third house in this row, to the west of Davis, was sold to Minerva Simons on January 18, 1844, for $140.[93] She had been born in Southbury, home of the Pootatuck band, in 1799, daughter of Cummy and Azuba.[94] Minerva was one of a number of Simonses from Southbury (South Britain village) who converged on Ethiope during the decade of the 1840s. Rachel Simons, widow of John, purchased land on Broad Street in 1846,[95] where her daughters Antoinette and Henrietta resided until their deaths two days apart during Christmas season in 1891.[96] And Mary Simons Pease, wife of John (John and Rachel's son), lived across the street from Minerva in the home of Eliza Hayes.[97] Members of the Simons family intermarried during this period with Peases, Cams and Starrs, all families referred to in various town histories as survivors of the Paugussett tribe.

To the west of Minerva Simons, at the corner of Main Street, the Stratfield Special School for Colored Children was built in 1845. On July 24 of that year the heirs of Aaron Hawley (1782–1801 overseer of the Golden Hill Indians) conveyed the lot for twenty-five dollars to Daniel Sterling and Silvanus Sterling of Bridgeport and Jesup Banks of Fairfield (all white citizens), "they being the Stratfield School Society Committee."[98] It was stipulated that the site "be held in trust forever for the purpose of permitting a School House to be built thereon for Colored Children." A second-story apartment may have been intended for the use of the schoolmaster (the earliest known was "E. Baker," listed in the 1855 *City Directory*; in 1857, it was John J.W. Baker, a twenty-one-year-old originally from New York). The 1855 *City Directory*, however, shows the living quarters occupied by "J. Hawley, seaman." The school building is presumed to have been removed to 188 Gregory Street in 1874 where it served as the home of Hugh Brady, P.T. Barnum's coachman.[99] It stood until destroyed by fire in July 2007.

The remaining portion of Whiting Street, between Main and Broad Streets, saw the construction of two more houses during this period. The more easterly plot was sold to William Allen on June 19, 1838.[100] Allen, a seaman formerly of Plattsville, Alabama, married Mary J. Porter (born in Maryland) on September 30, 1850.[101] An early twentieth-century article by Julian H. Sterling[102] relates, "Bill Allen [was] a famous character of those days, noted both as a soldier and a sailor. He was a giant in proportion, and fought pirates in the China Sea and served in the Civil War. He was one of those big fearless men ready for a fracas at a moment's notice, yet at heart as tender as a child. Any old timer who can remember 'Bill' will endorse this tribute to his memory."

To the west of Allen was a lot purchased by John Gowdy on July 26, 1839.[103] A house is shown here on the 1850 map, which in the 1855 *City Directory* is shown as occupied by William Thomas, seaman (born in Maryland). William Thomas was a trustee of Bethel Church in 1855. Of John Gowdy, no information has come to light—he is not in the Barbour Index of Connecticut Vital Records, the United States Census for

Connecticut for 1830, 1840 or 1850 and does not appear again in the grantor/grantee index of the Bridgeport Land Records under the name Gowdy or any variant of that spelling that has yet been conceived.

To the north of the original Zion Church on Broad Street, Simeon Dickson purchased a house from Ezra Gregory for $300 on May 11, 1841.[104] Dickson shortly afterward married Nancy Gibson of Bridgeport[105] "in the presence of (Rev.) Joshua Gibbs and Joel Freeman." Dickson is a thirty-four-year-old tailor on the September 25, 1850 birth record of his son, Alonzo Augustus; the census, taken on July 29 of that same year, lists him as a thirty-two-year-old cook. Dickson shared the house with the family of his brother-in-law Philander Pitts (married to Antoinette Gibson), sexton of Bridgeport's North Congregational Church and also named agent of Zion Church.[106] Pitts was one of the characters in Julian H. Sterling's historical novel *Space* (published in 1904), which deals with nineteenth-century Bridgeport.[107] One of Pitts's quotes reads: "They paid me for bell ringing and blowing the organ." Both wives are believed to be the daughters of Peter and Catherine Gibson of Southbury. A third Gibson woman (presumably Peter's sister), Roxy, was married to Rensselaer Pease in 1824.[108]

The young congregation of Zion Church experienced early growing pains. A doctrinal dispute arose, according to tradition, over the right of the clergyman to seek employment outside his ministry (in actuality, the dispute may have had more to do with cultural differences within the community). The larger part of the congregation left the smaller with the building but took the name of Zion Church. The smaller society became Ebeneezer and later Bethel Church. African Americans with roots in Maryland and other southern states all seemed to affiliate with Bethel Church (William H. Davis being the sole exception encountered), while those from Connecticut and New York State with known or likely Native American antecedents were consistently linked to Zion Church. Land was procured two hundred feet to the north on Broad Street on May 20, 1843, and construction of Zion's more commodious structure commenced at once. Historian Hurd took note of a tablet over the door of the newer building with an inscription from the Old Testament: "The glory of the latter house shall exceed that of the former." In Hurd's day (1881), Zion Church had eighty-two members, with a Sunday school of seventy; Bethel Church had twenty-eight members, with a Sunday school of twenty.

In conjunction with the churches, the place of burial for community inhabitants—or, rather, the lack of any records of such interments—should be mentioned. For the first half-century after the founding of Zion Church, graves of only two members of the Ethiope community—Grant Hawley (Lakeview Cemetery) and Edward A. Jackson (Mountain Grove Cemetery)—were found in the statewide burial index in Bridgeport. It is known that Mary and Eliza Freeman, sisters of Joel, were returned for burial to their hometown of Derby. But Joel Freeman, John Johnson, Tunis Green, Presence Jackson, John Feeley, Simeon Dixon and the Deming family—all of whom presumably had the wherewithal to procure a headstone—are nowhere to be found. After the 1880s, however, burials of Ethiope residents are almost universally to be found in established local cemeteries. It may be that, in common with many A.M.E. Churches,

Bethel and Zion had a small graveyard close by the church buildings that became abandoned in later years and was subsequently forgotten.

Construction of homes in the village picked up as the local economy rebounded. Ezra Gregory appears to have engaged himself to the construction of a double house directly to the north of Zion Church while that edifice was under construction. He sold the south half to Salisbury Lane on November 4, 1843,[109] and the north half to Samuel Serrington[110] on March 30, 1844. As noted in the 1855 *City Directory*, the south half was the home to Edward Hubbell, whose household included Hamilton and Olive Pease Jackson (known Paugussett) in the 1860 census. Across the street, at the northeast corner of Broad and Whiting Streets, Edward A. Jackson of New York City purchased a lot on August 15, 1845, for $220 and began construction of a house.[111] Jackson, listed in the 1850 census as a waiter, died on September 15, 1851, at age thirty-one. His rather ambitious Greek Revival residence was removed early in the twentieth century and stands today at 372 Gregory Street. To the north of Jackson and opposite Zion Church, another double house was built by Sherwood Sterling at about the same time. The north half was sold on September 11, 1846, to William Johnson of New York City, and the south half to George W. Francis, operator of a variety store at 18 Wall Street in Bridgeport's city center.[112] He appears to have been the father of Reverend Timothy Francis, pastor of Bethel Church in 1870.

Clearly, by the mid-1840s the village limits of Ethiope needed to expand beyond the immediate orbit of Broad and Whiting Streets. Main Street had been extended to the south in 1841.[113] To meet the increasing demand for lots, Ezra Gregory began selling his land to the west of both churches along what would become Gregory Street (referred to as such for a number of years after houses had been constructed here, however, it was still referred to in deeds as the "contemplated street"). Proceeding west from Zion Church, lot purchasers were William Allen,[114] Harry Morris,[115] and Grant and Maria Hawley.[116] All these transactions took place between 1845 and 1850. William Allen, seaman, was discussed previously in connection with his earlier home on Whiting Street. Harry Morris, a gardener born in the town of Huntington, married Mary Thorn on April 11, 1842.[117] His property was later sold to Eliza Freeman in 1852,[118] and her brother Joel also obtained an interest. Grant Hawley (born 1801) was one of the founding trustees of Zion Church. He died on October 12, 1855; his widow Maria continued to reside on the property they had purchased from Gregory until her death on February 10, 1899.

7.

Ethiope Becomes Liberia

Major changes were in the offing as the decade of the 1840s progressed. The New York and New Haven Railroad, which would put Bridgeport within a ninety-minute radius of the metropolis, was to open in 1848, and a flood of new employment opportunities in business and industry would follow. Again, Ethiope would participate in Bridgeport's progress. By 1850, the census counted 7,558 residents in the city, with 286 listed as "colored" (none, of course, were labeled Indian).

Ethiope as a name for the locale is found in deeds prior to this time,[119] and marriage records have been found[120] where the individuals are referred to as "Ethiopis." The *Britannica World Language Dictionary* contains the word Ethiop, an "archaic adjective," and states it is derived from the Latin "Aethiops," in turn derived from the Greek "Aithops," a combination of aithein (burn) and ops (face).

This cognomen may have been considered a pejorative by the village's inhabitants. Whatever the reason, by the 1850s, deeds[121] describe the locale as "a place called Liberia." The timing of this change appears to have approximately coincided with the African nation's independence in 1847, and the new name would have underscored the sense of freedom the residents felt in their newly ascendant community. Southern Connecticut may have felt an especial kinship to Liberia in Africa, as Jehudi Ashmun (1794–1828), a white American regarded as the founder of that nation in 1822, spent the last portion of his life in New Haven, seventeen miles from Bridgeport.

The climate in Bridgeport's Liberia in this period is suggested in an item that appeared in the *Republican Farmer* on October 1, 1849:

> *Colored People's Library*
>
> *The colored people's Elevation Society, of this city, have undertaken to get up a library, for their moral and educational improvement, and desire the assistance of our white citizens in their laudable enterprise. For this purpose they have appointed Mrs. Francis, Miss Bloomfield, Miss Huested, Mrs. Hubbard, and Miss Brown, to solicit contributions of such books as*

their white friends may be pleased to make. Books may also be left with either the Rev. R. [sic] *Collins, George W. Francis, or J. Emory Burr, who are duly appointed Library Committee.*

Those of our citizens who have useful books which they can spare without serious inconvenience to themselves cannot, we are sure, make a better use of them, than by appropriating them to this society.

The library appears to have been connected with Zion Church. In the 1871–72 *City Directory,*[122] in a list of church officers, Jacob Pelham's occupation is listed as librarian.

By the late '40s, the land on the east side of Main Street to the north of Whiting Street was added to Liberia's built-up area. In 1847, Moses[123] and Eliza Martin Hayes[124] purchased a lot and dwelling house.[125] Earlier, in 1839, they had purchased a lot at Newfield from Captain Henry Burroughs.[126] As discussed earlier, Eliza "kept the old Knickerbocker House corner Wall and Water Streets, and was well known by all our old residents."[127] Notably, these residents were not merely persons of color.

To the north and west of the Hayes house, lots were purchased and houses constructed the following year for Mary and Eliza Freeman, the two sisters of Joel Freeman (and thus Turkey Hill Paugussetts). To judge from their known attainments, and from the record of their lives in newspaper accounts and public documents, they must have been among the most eminent of Liberia's nineteenth-century inhabitants. Among the community's antebellum houses, theirs alone survive to the present time on their original foundations and are enrolled today in the National Register of Historic Places (in which, however, the women are erroneously described as African Americans, a result of my mistaken assumption regarding the word colored).

Mary Freeman (1815–1883) and Eliza Freeman (1805–1862) appear to have remained unmarried throughout their lifetimes. They lived in Derby until about the time of their mother's death in 1843. One land record[128] states that they are "of said Derby" in 1842, but names both of them "of the city and state of New York" two years later.[129] Mary "act[ed] in the capacity of cook in a New York hotel"[130] during this period.

On April 11, 1848, the sisters sold the family holdings at Derby consisting of a six-acre and thirteen-acre parcel for the sum of $700.[131] On May 5 of the same year, Mary purchased a building lot around the corner from Joel's homestead[132] for $150. On September 12, 1848, she refinanced the property "with buildings thereon standing,"[133] and on that same day, her sister Eliza bought the lot adjoining to the south.[134]

For a few years the Freeman sisters seem to have utilized their homes as rental properties while they worked and resided in New York. The beginning of railroad passenger service between New York and Bridgeport the same year that the houses were constructed may have facilitated this arrangement. Some time before 1855, Eliza moved to Bridgeport, and around 1858 she took employment in the home of Catherine Maria Bassett, whose husband, Captain Freeman C. Bassett, had died that year. The 1860 census credits Eliza with real estate valued at $3,000 (in addition to her own home, she owned a half interest—with her brother Joel—in a block of three

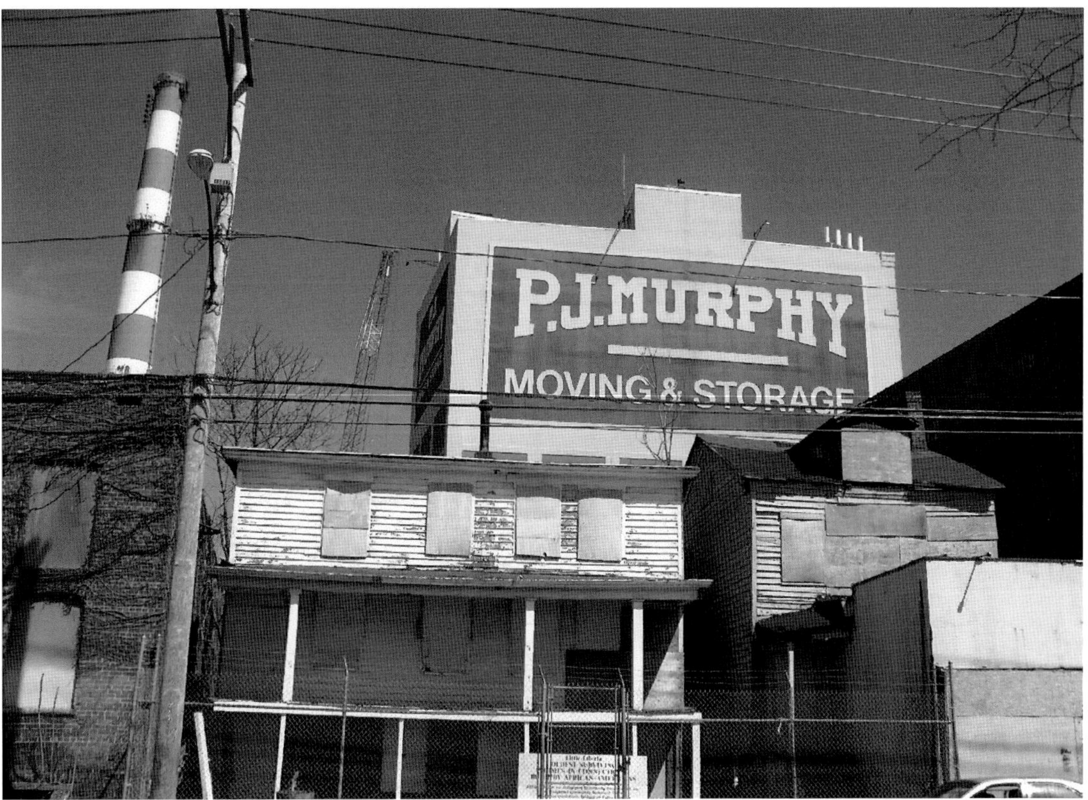

The Mary Freeman (left) and Eliza Freeman (right) Houses stand in deteriorated condition on Main Street between Kiefer and Whiting Streets.

tenements at 16–18 Gregory Street). Her household was shared in that year with four other women, all of whom had been born in Connecticut: Sarah Freeman, aged fifty-eight;[135] Catherine Purdy, aged fifty;[136] Sally Roberts, aged fifty-five; and Sernia Freeman, aged forty-five. In the 1862 *City Directory* her companions at 76 Main Street were Cornelia Sauls and Lucy Starr. These family surnames have all been attached to the Paugussett tribe in various sources.

Eliza Freeman died July 19, 1862, at the age of fifty-six. An inventory of her possessions at that time[137] suggests the attainment of solid middle-class respectability, with perhaps an unusually fine wardrobe. Mary Freeman had also come to Bridgeport prior to her sister's death, and she subsequently bought out Joel's interest in Eliza's properties. By the time of the 1870 census, where she is enumerated as "Jane Freeman," her real estate was valued at $10,000 and her personal estate at $2,000.

We know a few of Mary Freeman's achievements in the ensuing decades. She sold off Joel's property for $2,500 to be demolished for a new Naugatuck Railroad freight yard in 1870.[138] Mary Freeman took instruction and was baptized as a member of the First Methodist Episcopal Church of Bridgeport in 1858 (records indicate that she transferred to another church in 1872—in the 1862 *City Directory*, her tenant at 80

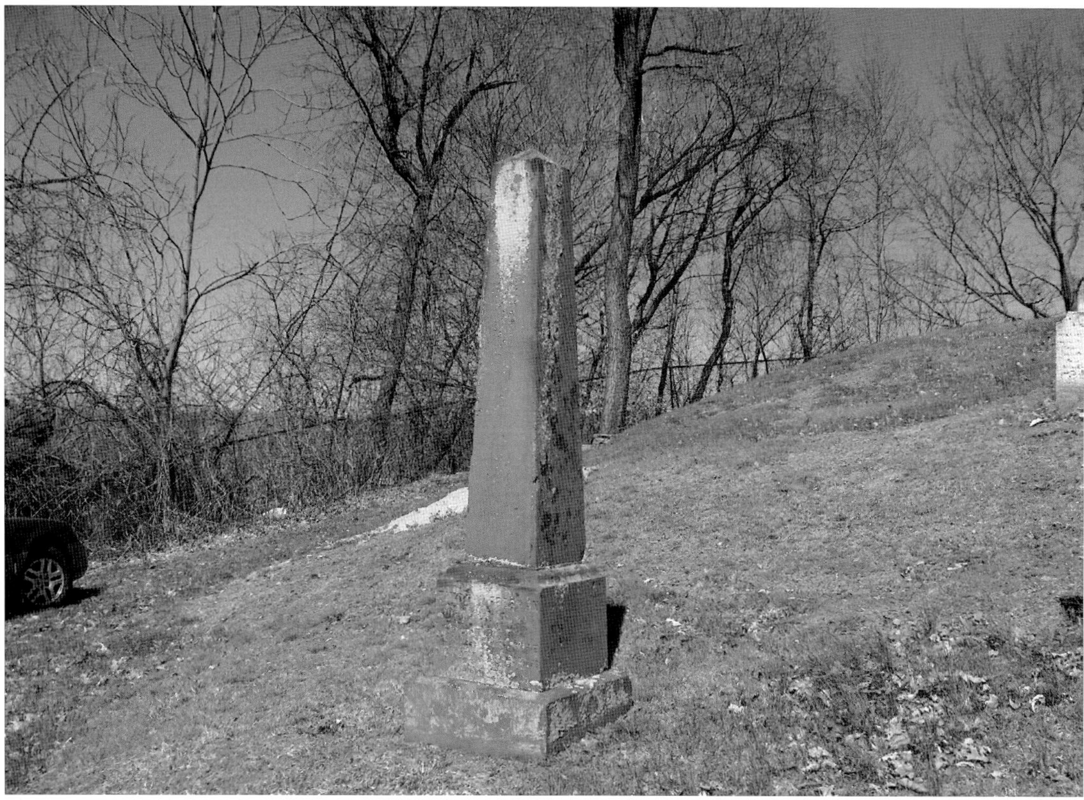

The monument Mary Freeman had placed over the grave of her parents in the 1840s and where Eliza was buried, Uptown Derby Burial Ground.

Main Street was Reverend Charles L. Fowler, pastor of Bethel Church). Mary placed an eight-foot brownstone monument of obelisk form over the graves of her parents and sister in the Uptown Derby Burial Ground, giving the family plot prominence in the cemetery. And, as if in deference, she was habitually listed in the Bridgeport city directories as Miss Mary Freeman, a courteous distinction afforded no other woman of color enumerated.

A somewhat contrasting view of Mary's character is painted by an article in the *Bridgeport Standard* on January 1, 1882. It describes the horrendous death of her seventy-five-year-old tenant, Chloe Hawley:

> *About quarter of ten o'clock, Saturday night, an alarm of fire was sounded, from box 43, corner of Main and Kiefer Streets. The department turned out promptly and the chemical speedily extinguished the fire which was in the house, in the rear of 114 Main Street. The house was occupied by Mrs. David Hawley, an aged colored woman, and the fire started in a bed. Some of the neighbors discovered the fire, and on entering the room found Mrs. Hawley lying in the flames. She was removed as quickly as possible, and carried out doors. William Craw, driver of number 5's hose, drove rapidly after Dr. Cumming, and carried him to the fire in the hose cart. On making an examination he found that the unfortunate woman was*

probably fatally injured. One arm was charred badly, and she was also burned on the breast. Her clothing was nearly all consumed, and she had inhaled the smoke and flame, causing internal injuries. She was taken to the residence of Mrs. Charles Hubbard, but nothing could be done for her. She died several hours later. The origin of the fire could not be ascertained, but it is thought that a burning candle ignited some clothing on the wall, as a candle was found on the floor. Some of the colored people were very indignant, because the woman who owned the house and lived close by refused to allow the unfortunate woman to be carried into her house. The deceased was at one time a slave, and must have been very old but her age is not known. She has a son and has been engaged in laundry work, and was frequently seen drawing her clothes basket around on a small cart. The remains were removed to the undertaking rooms of Bishop & Cullinan and prepared for burial. Sunday afternoon a jury of inquest met before Justice J.P. Pinkerman and examined a number of witnesses and adjourned to two o'clock yesterday afternoon, when several witnesses were examined. The evidence did not show how the fire originated, but the statements of the witnesses deepened the feeling against the woman who closed her doors against the deceased, and some members of the jury expressed a desire to allude to her conduct in the verdict. It was finally decided that it did not properly belong to them to do so. The jury rendered a verdict in accordance with the facts.

On March 14, 1883, the *Bridgeport Standard* carried the following item:

Miss Mary Freeman, an old and well known colored lady, died at her residence at 114 Main Street yesterday of intermittent fever. The deceased was sixty-eight years of age, and had during her life accumulated considerable property, which is variously estimated at from $30,000 to $50,000. She owned several houses on Main and Gregory Streets.

Mary's will[139] provides evidence of financial attainments unusual for Native American women in the nineteenth century, including reference to her "large cottage known as the Hillman Cottage, at Sea Cliff, Long Island." She requested "a decent burial as near the place of my deceased mother in a burial ground in the town of Derby in New Haven County, as may be suitable and convenient and within a reasonable time thereafter, to cause to be inscribed upon a monument I have erected upon the ground aforesaid my name with the time of my birth and death."

Mary's will that named as executor the Reverend Albert Nash, pastor of the First Methodist Episcopal Church of Bridgeport in 1860–61 and executor of Joel's estate in 1865, was revoked on March 12, 1883, the day prior to her death. A new will, witnessed by three close white neighbors, was substituted, which named her physician, Dr. Arthur Almon Holmes (1839–1910),[140] as executor as well as primary beneficiary (one other heir was Mary Jane Cam Brown, Mary Freeman's servant).[141] Within a year, Holmes moved from Bridgeport to the upstate resort community of Lakeville. Perhaps significantly, Mary's name was never inscribed on the family monument in Derby.

Mary Freeman's brother Franklin, a resident of Boston and Chelsea, Massachusetts, filed suit to overturn the second will. His claims were apparently of sufficient merit to

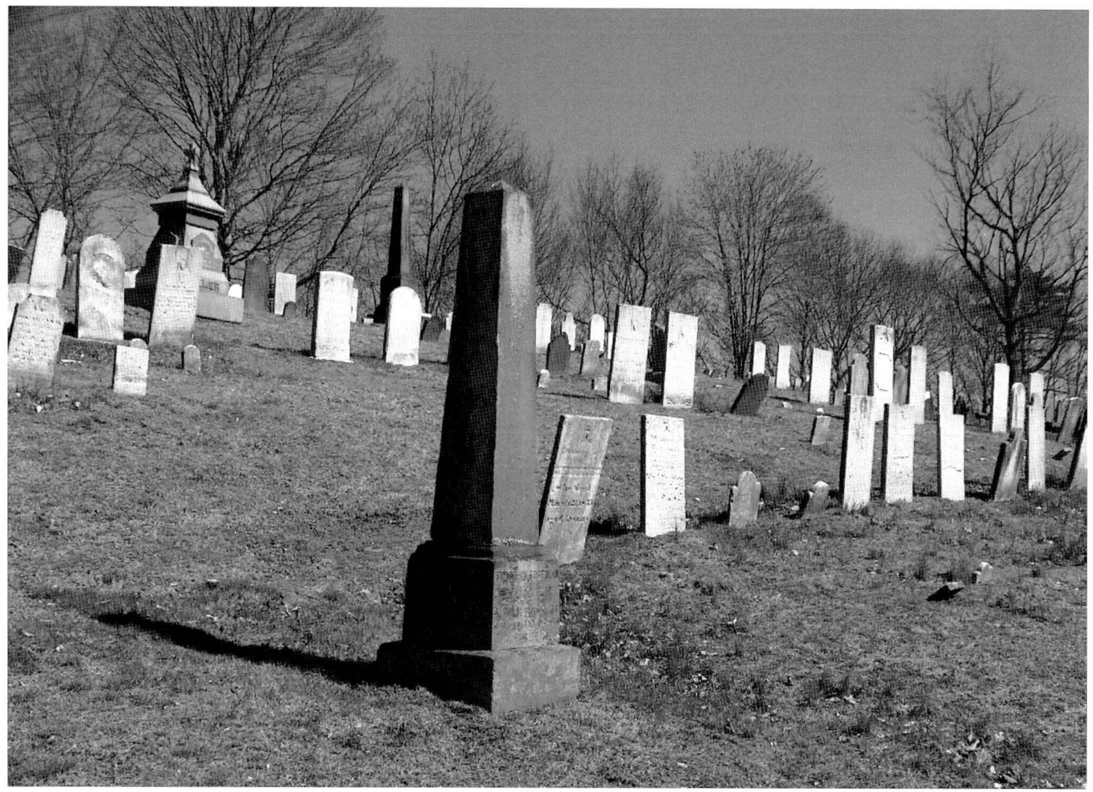

The side of the monument reserved for Mary's name remains blank to this day.

enable him to obtain a mortgage against two of Mary's properties in the amount of $4,000 on December 15, 1888,[142] although the case had not yet been adjudicated. It may be that these funds were needed during his last illness, for in the next recorded transaction in Bridgeport Land Records (May 23, 1889) he is noted as deceased.[143]

Mary appears to have had an ongoing association with the Reverend Nash that extended long after he departed his Bridgeport congregation in 1861 and moved on to charges in East Norwalk, Connecticut, and Brooklyn, New York. As a man of some property, with $5,000 in real estate in the 1860 census, it is possible that he may have served as her financial as well as spiritual advisor. The 1870 census shows John Nash, his son, as a resident in Mary's household. By 1889 Reverend Nash was seventy-seven years of age, retired and living in Otego, New York, located 204 miles from Bridgeport. For reasons unknown, he borrowed funds and purchased the Mary and Eliza Freeman houses on May 23 of that year.[144] He continued to reside in Otego until his death on May 14, 1900, and apparently rented out the properties.

Perhaps the houses may have been kept as places of refuge for people of color in need. This is suggested by a pair of articles that appeared in the *Bridgeport Standard* shortly before and shortly after Mary Freeman's death. The first, "Kidnapped and Outraged,"[145] describes the abduction, brutalization and rape of six-year-old Lena, the daughter of Mr. A.B. Ruby. The second entry, "The Thunder Storm,"[146] reports a lightning strike and the resultant damage at Mary's house. The occupant at that time was the same A.B. Ruby.

There were apparently restrictive covenants on some of Liberia's property deeds. On January 4, 1853, for example, William A. Dowd, a white man, sold a house and lot on the south side of Gregory Street nearly opposite Zion Church to John Elsey (also spelled Elzey) of Bridgeport for $500.[147] The deed stipulated:

> *One condition, however, and it is hereby understood & agreed by and between said William A. Dowd and said John Elzey, their heirs, executors, administrators, and assigns, and the heirs' executors, administrators, & assigns of each of them in consideration of said conveyance, that the said John Elzey shall under no circumstances sell, assign, mortgage, convey, lease, or permit to occupy or possess said premises in any manner or form any White person or persons, except said William A. Dowd or any institution or corporation composed of white persons without the permission or consent of said William A. Dowd, or his heirs, executors, or administrators, under the penalty of the reversion of said premises, on such sale, occupation, or possession to said William A. Dowd, his heirs, executors, or assigns.*

William A. Dowd had purchased land at Waltersville in 1845 and constructed a combination business/residential structure.[148] Orcutt names him as the mason in charge of construction on the North Congregational Church in 1847.[149] He is listed in both the 1855 and 1857 *City Directory* as the proprietor of an "Eating Saloon" at 5 Bank Street, with his residence next door. There are no indications of what might have led him to place this clause on the property's title.[150]

What was perhaps the high point in Liberia's physical development occurred in the summer of 1853. Alexander Duncan[151] had purchased a house at the northeast corner of Main and Whiting Streets for $1,200 in 1840.[152] An 1847 mortgage note from Minott Mitchell of White Plains[153] shows that he also owned property in Albany; his New York City holding is described as being "on Laurens Street[154] between Grand and Canal Streets."

On April 8, 1853, Duncan obtained a $1,331 mortgage from the Bridgeport Mutual Savings Bank and Building Association, and began either the new construction or the remodeling of the earlier structure into the Duncan House Hotel. The building stood until 1924, and old photographs show it to have been a wooden, three-story, Italianate-style structure with a high English basement and a monitor roof. It included an ornate wraparound veranda and faced Whiting Street and the waters of Bridgeport's outer harbor. Construction appears to have been mostly completed by December of that year.[155]

Possible connections in New York City between Duncan and Mary Freeman, who resided just to the north of the hotel, have not been explored. Duncan added a "barn or store house" in 1855, when he is described as "now living in Bridgeport, Connecticut,"[156] and engaged in a dispute with Eliza Hayes over the location of a property boundary.[157]

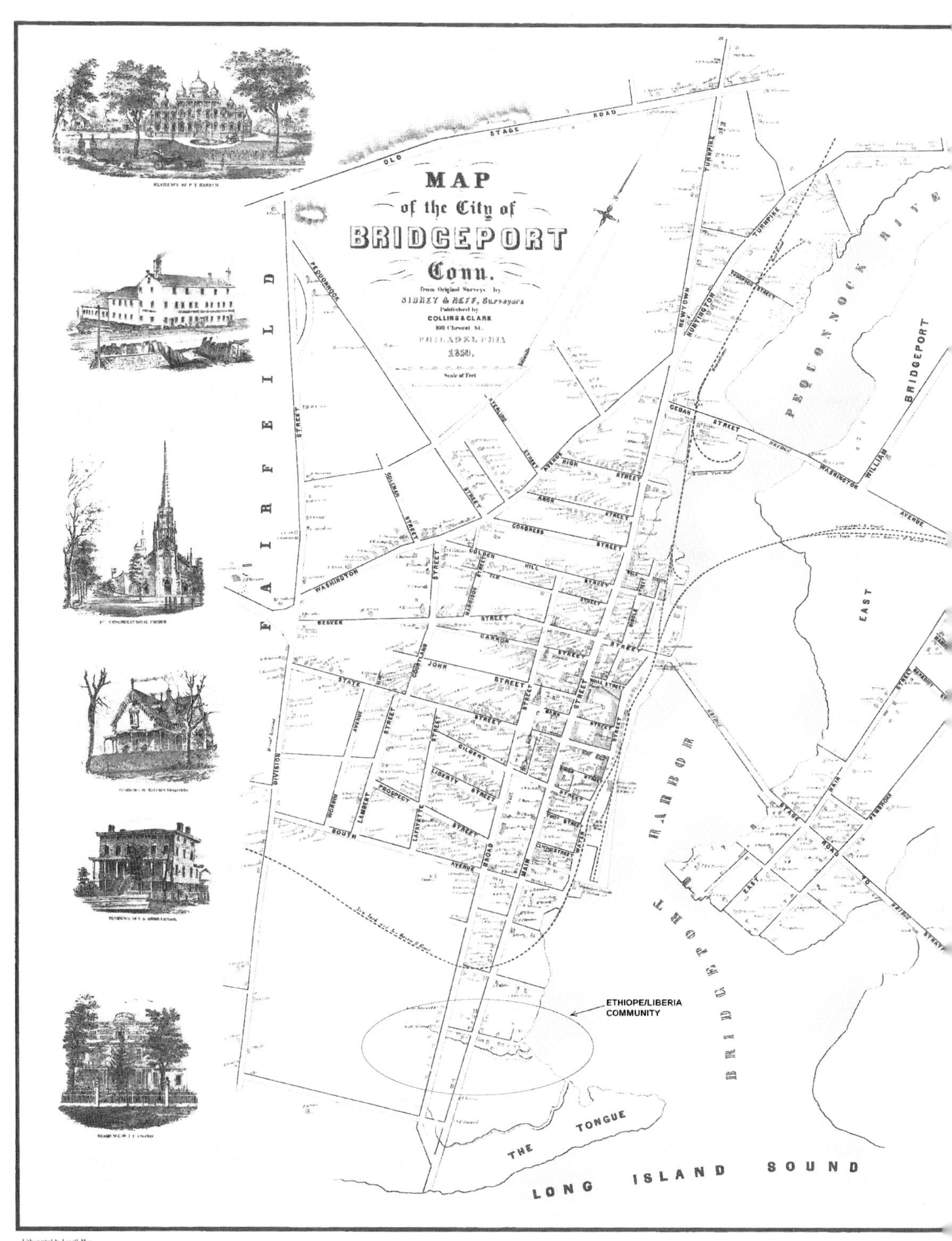
MAP
of the City of
BRIDGEPORT
Conn.
from Original Surveys by
SIDNEY & NEFF, Surveyors
Published by
COLLINS & CLARK
PHILADELPHIA
1850.
Scale of Feet
OLD STAGE ROAD
FAIRFIELD
PEQUONNOCK RIVER
BRIDGEPORT
EAST
BRIDGEPORT HARBOR
THE TONGUE
LONG ISLAND SOUND
ETHIOPE/LIBERIA
COMMUNITY
TURNPIKE
NEWTOWN
HUNTINGTON
CEDAR STREET
WASHINGTON
WILLIAM
AVENUE
HIGH STREET
ARCH STREET
CONGRESS STREET
GOLDEN HILL STREET
BEAVER
CANNON STREET
JOHN STREET
STATE STREET
DIVISION
GILBERT STREET
LIBERTY STREET
PROSPECT
SOUTH AVENUE
BROAD
MAIN
WATER
LAFAYETTE
LAMBERT
STAGE ROAD

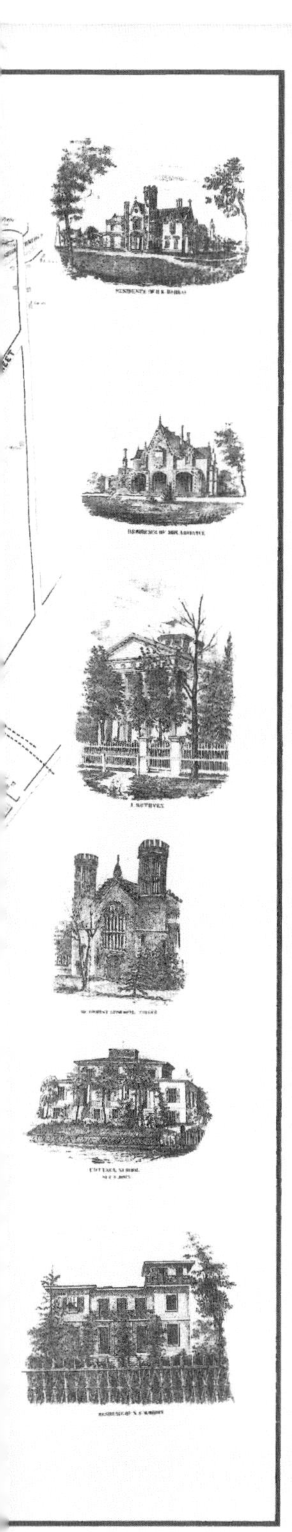

The 1855 *City Directory* lists "Duncan House Hotel, cor. Main & Whiting, Alexander Duncan, col'd., proprietor."

The hotel was a major economic impetus for the Liberia community, and a number of its inhabitants were soon employed as cooks, waitstaff, and other personnel. It is probable that fishing and agricultural interests in the rural sector were also stimulated by this new venture.

Duncan may have been overextended by construction costs, however, because he sold the hotel to John Douglas of Brooklyn, New York (born in Pennsylvania), on April 25, 1855.[158] Douglas is enumerated at the premises in the 1860 census and the 1862 *City Directory* lists him as the resident "col'd." hotel keeper.

A perusal of 1850 and 1860 census records and city directories for the antebellum period show that the men of the Liberia community comprised the bulk of those Bridgeport residents listed as seamen and had a virtual monopoly in the city on the trades of barber and waiter. Similarly, the women monopolized the occupation of laundress or washerwoman. Both genders found employment as steamboat cooks.

Liberia as developed in 1850—note that house owners' names are not included, demarcating the community from the rest of the city. *Map courtesy of the Historical Collections, Bridgeport Public Library.*

8.

The Golden Hill Indians at Trumbull

The conditions of the indigent Indians who were claimants on the Golden Hill Tribal Fund stood in stark contrast to that of the strivers of Liberia. Located less than eight miles to the northeast in the village of Nichols Farms, the 19¾-acre Wells Turnpike tract had been purchased for their use in 1842 under the auspices of overseer Smith Tweedy.[159] Tweedy was an elderly hat manufacturer who had moved to Bridgeport from Danbury. He may have been intrigued by the Brook Farm experiment underway in Massachusetts that same year and hoped that the welfare clients in his charge could, through communal effort at "healthy" farm labor, become productive members of society like their brethren in the city just to the south. The reason behind the choice of a location at Nichols Farms is not known—Tweedy may have been acquainted with Franklin Ambler, the most important citizen of that place, who was likewise a Danbury native.

Like Brook Farm, the Wells Turnpike endeavor apparently did not work out as had been hoped. Accounts—all, of course, written by white observers with their inherent bias—tell of indolence, drunkenness and debauchery, culminating in the destruction by arson of an almost-new barn. The common-law spouse of one of the native women ("they live in irregular connection with Negroes" was one of the invectives leveled by DeForest during this period, a serious affront to mainstream Victorian-era mores) would spend the remainder of his life in state prison for this offense.

Finally, in 1854, the new overseer, Dwight Morris, put an end to the experiment and sold off the land, claiming the Indians did not manage it well. Morris (1816–1894) was a prominent Bridgeport attorney known for his temperance stance and his "dignified and military bearing."[160]

William Sherman had married the preceding year, and he moved to the community of Nichols Farms from Bridgeport around 1857. He appears to have been instilled with a strong work ethic—whether through his employment on whaling ships, his experience in the Bridgeport community or from Morris's sale of the land base, inculcating him with the message "sink or swim," it is impossible to state. He records dealings with Morris in his journal (i.e. "A Count William Sherman and Dwight Morris...in 1857 receive $9.00 for Henry Pease"). He has other dealings—hay deliveries and such[161]—with Gideon Thompson (Tomsen), Morris's father-in-law. It should be noted that Morris purchased Lindencroft, the Bridgeport mansion of P.T. Barnum, in 1869.[162]

The sketch of William Sherman that appeared in Orcutt's *History of Stratford and Bridgeport* of 1886 was, we now know, the contribution of Richard C. Ambler (1853–1891), son of Charles and grandson of Franklin P. Ambler (Sherman's employer and patron).[163] Richard Ambler was the curator of the Fairfield County Historical Society,[164] and he also supplied the material contained in Hurd's *History of Fairfield County* (1881) regarding Sherman. This reads in part, "William Sherman, the most intelligent of their number, lives in the town of Trumbull. He has for many years been in the employ of the Ambler family, by whom he is held in very high esteem for his many good qualities."

Orcutt's history provides us with additional information:

> [He] *was a sailor in a whaling ship seventeen years; and has been 'round the world nine times; was first mate of the ship five years and earned an honorable standing and reputation, which he has retained to the present time. He educated himself, and could perform the services of a first mate on a vessel correctly as well as intelligently. He has long been a respected farm laborer at Nichols Farms, and long trusted with considerable responsibility in the management of the farm and properties of Mr. F.P. Ambler and sons.*

A description of Sherman that appeared in a June 13, 1937 newspaper article echoes Julian Sterling's description of William Allen. The article states: "Anybody who saw him in the latter part of his life was not likely to forget him for he weighed 360 pounds...[He] was the original visiting nurse of Fairfield County. He is remembered as having been a perfect attendant upon the sick, because in spite of his great strength he could be as gentle as a lamb."

Sherman had a very close relationship with Franklin Ambler, supremely exemplified in his journal entry for July 28, 1873, which reads: "Went to take care of the Old Man and stayed with him until he died August 1." Franklin Ambler was a saddletree manufacturer, and his business was so successful that Nichols Farms became known as Amblersville during the Civil War era. Ambler was born in 1797 in Danbury and spent the early years of his career in Derby. "The early life of Franklin P. Ambler was one of poverty and hardship, through which he struggled with undaunted courage," we read in Hurd's history. It continues:

> *Franklin P. Ambler had during his boyhood little opportunity for education, but was always an enthusiastic reader; remarkable for an exceedingly retentive memory, he soon acquired a knowledge difficult to be competed with. To this he constantly made additions until in middle and later life he was able to converse, with equal intelligence, with those of far greater opportunities. ...Gifted with a powerful and retentive memory, he seldom forgot anything of importance that he read, and, always from his youth up an industrious reader, his mind was stored with a fund of facts, anecdotes, and historical information from which he would at*

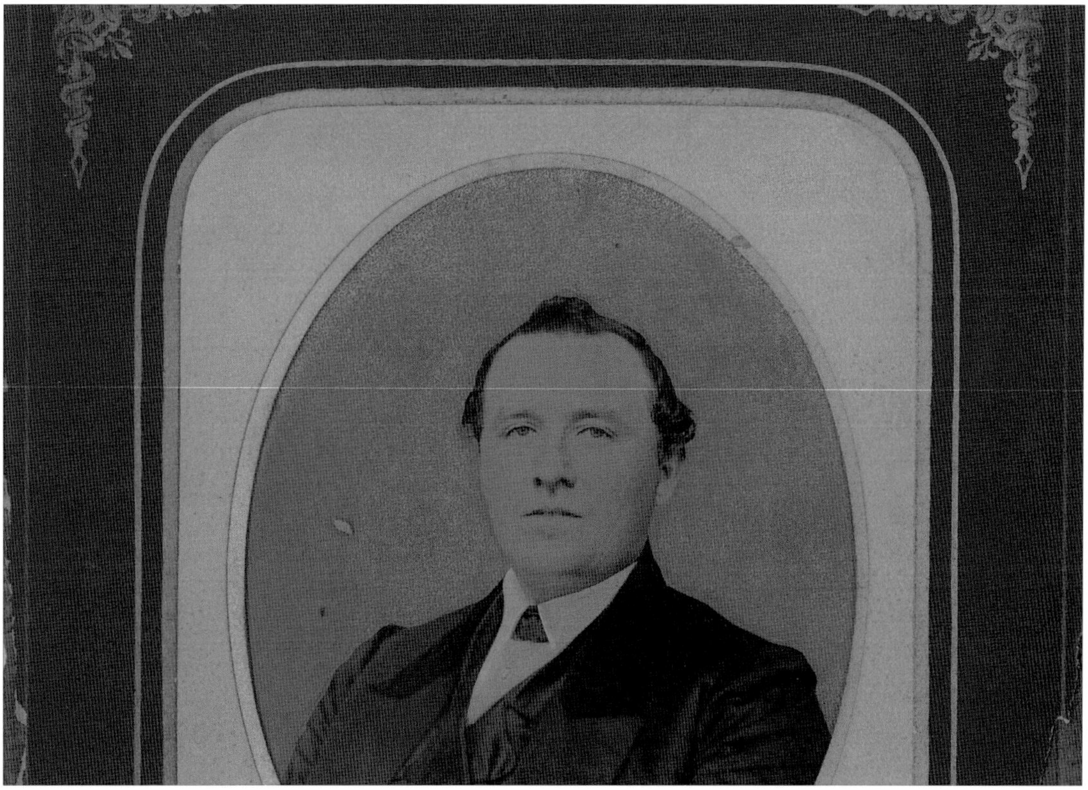

Franklin Ambler. *Courtesy of the Trumbull Historical Society.*

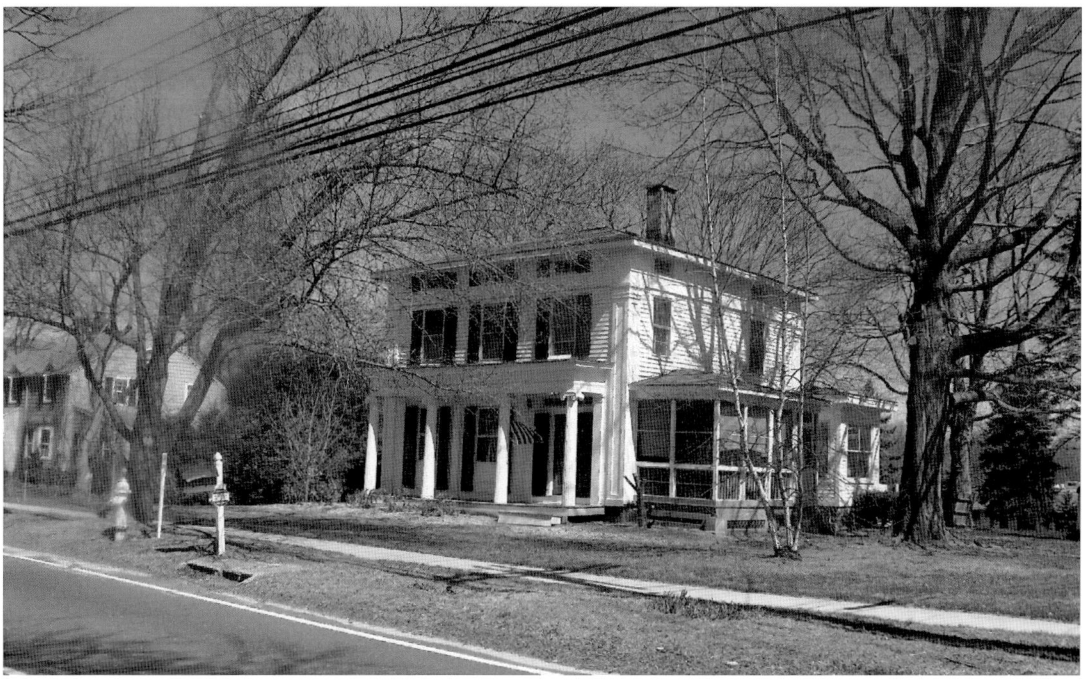

Franklin Ambler's house in Nichols.

pleasure draw to enliven, strengthen, and adorn his naturally easy conversation. He had accumulated a solid and valuable library, and his peculiar qualities of mind made his books almost literally reproduced in him.

Describing his offspring, Hurd adds, "In speaking of them one cannot but associate them together, for it was together, the father and the three sons, that every one meant when they spoke of the 'Amblers.'"

Of the sons, Charles Ambler[165] alone survived until the time William Sherman began recording his daily activities in some detail in April 1873. Charles is perhaps the most frequently mentioned personage in the journal, and it is clear that the men were friends in addition to being employer and employee (e.g. "went to Bridgeport with Charles Ambler," April 1, 1873; "went a-clamming with Charles Ambler," September 24, 1874). Charles was one of the "inner circle" who socialized with the Shermans on Sundays, and, perhaps most poignantly, accompanied William on the wagon ride to Bridgeport to procure a coffin the day William's baby died. Clearly, this family being the source of historical information regarding Sherman adds much weight to its credence and import.

9.

The James Farm Community

Two miles east of Nichols Farms was the fourth predominantly Paugussett community in the vicinity of Bridgeport. James Farm was actually a series of farmsteads atop a long, high ridge (Prospect Hill on an 1867 map) that overlooked the wide Housatonic River and its salt-meadow margins. James Farm was located nine and a half miles northeast of Liberia and six and a half miles southwest of Derby, close by the boundaries of Huntington and Trumbull townships.

Marcus B. Freeman[166] resided here at the time of the 1820 census, as did Benjamin Freeman, who moved to Ethiope in 1825. Both appear to have descended from the prolific Edwards clan, and they may in fact have been brothers. Marcus (or Mark) was the father of another important personage in William Sherman's journal, George Freeman (1816–1888). George's 1846 farmhouse still stands on James Farm Road opposite Peter's Lane, two miles southeast of William Sherman's homestead. The fields and woodlots surrounding it have survived remarkably intact (Stratford today is almost entirely urbanized, with a population density of 2,500 people per square mile), bordered by extensive stone fencing comprised almost solely of boulders. Viewing the product of George's labor it becomes comprehensible why Stratford death records[167] show his cause of death as "exhaustion."

George's obituary[168] states that he was "known far and wide as Yellow George." It continues, "He was a man of considerable influence among all classes in his neighborhood, and was one of the most successful shad fishermen on the river and had accumulated considerable property." In 1866, Stratford Land Records indicate that he had acquired 2/20 interest in the Friar's Head Fishing Place, and 3/24 interest in the Oronoque Meadow Fishing Place that bordered it to the north.[169] Shad swim up major northeastern rivers like the Housatonic to spawn for a few weeks in the early spring, and their flesh and broiled roe were a fashionable entrée in Victorian-era dining salons. A frequent notation in William Sherman's journal was "went atsom shad" and "went a-shadding." As Freeman's fishing grounds were the closest point on the river to Sherman's residence, this wording may have been a synonym for spending time with his friend George.

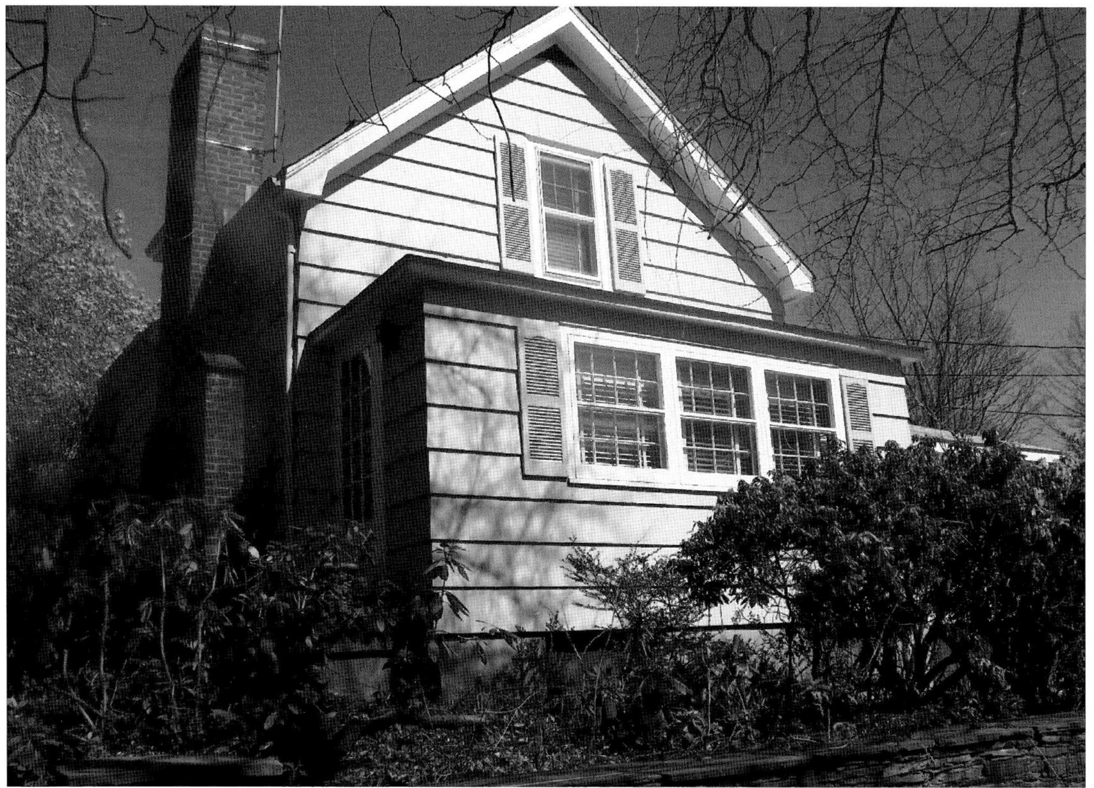

George Freeman's house on James Farm Road.

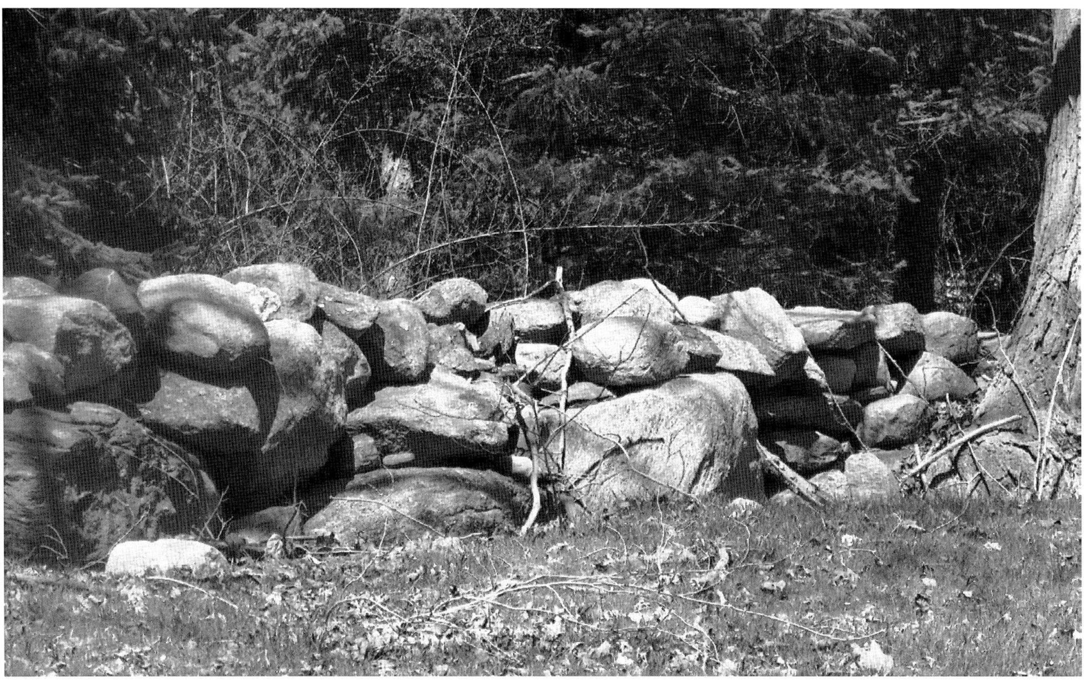

George Freeman's stone walls.

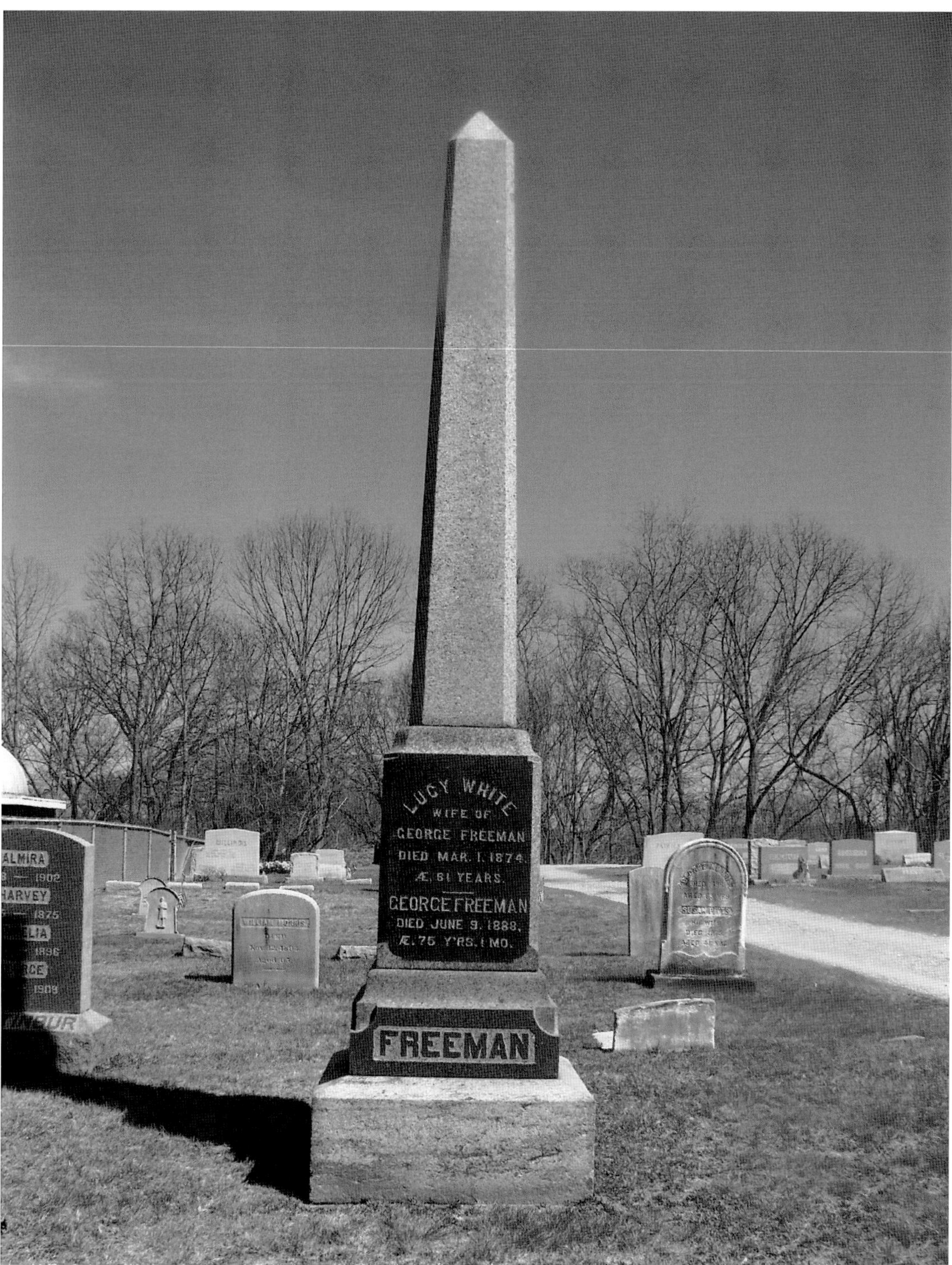

George Freeman's monument, Putney Cemetery, Stratford.

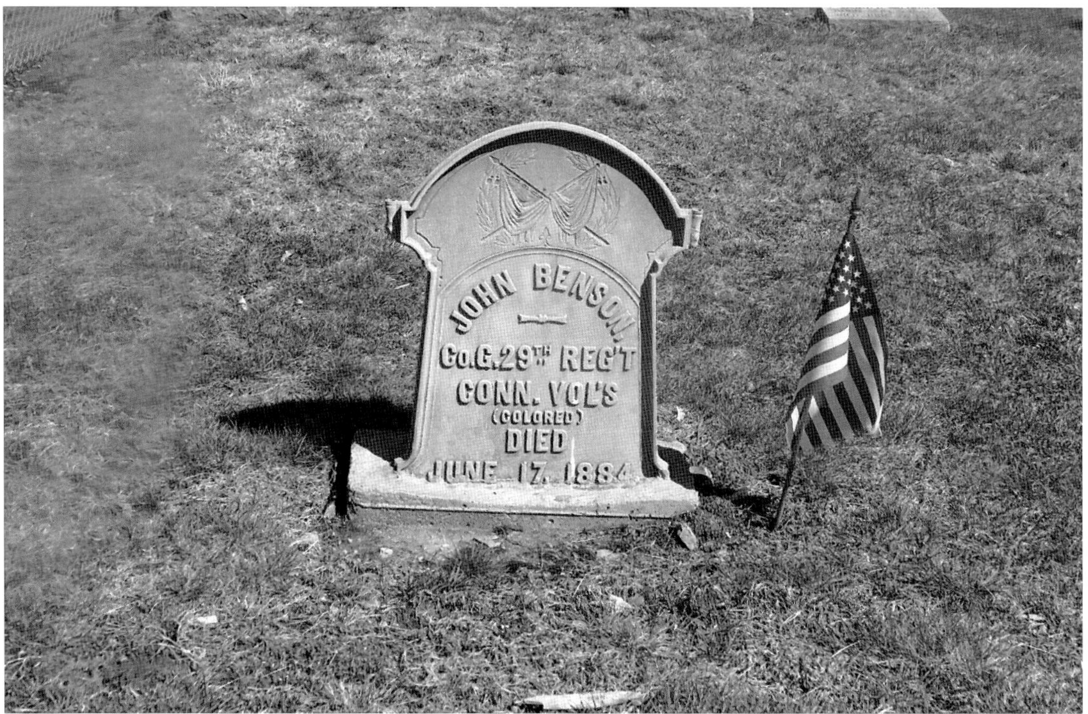

John Benson's grave marker.

Other families in this community, which gathered mostly in the period 1841–46, included the Martinburghs and the Whites, both repeatedly mentioned in the Sherman journal. Marcus B. Freeman had married Venus Thomas of Bridgeport on August 13, 1840, his second marriage,[170] so Sherman's entry "went to Putney and got Venus" becomes meaningful. George married Lucy White on November 21, 1839.[171] Their son Theodore (born 1851) died relatively young, and Sherman attended his funeral.[172] George had a brother, Edwin,[173] who resided in Bridgeport in the Newfield community.

Lucy's brother Boston White, as well as Edwin Freeman and John Benson (brother of Janette Benson who was to marry Henry O. Pease), enlisted together in the Twenty-ninth Connecticut Colored Infantry in January 1864, and mustered out together in October 1865. They were later buried together in George Freeman's plot in Putney Cemetery. George's burial plot bears a striking resemblance to William Sherman's in Nichols Farms. He had purchased the eight-and-a-half- by thirty-three-foot plot for ten dollars on September 20, 1876.[174] The Freemans' large granite monument (similar in form to Mary Freeman's in the cemetery at Derby) is toward the front, and behind it are the smaller headstones of the Martinburghs, Whites and John Benson.

In another part of North Stratford called Second Hill, three miles to the southwest of James Farm and practically on the outskirts of Nichols Farms village, was the farming operation of Ransom D. Curtis, brother-in-law of Franklin Ambler, whose primary employment was also as a saddletree maker. William Sherman's journal shows that he performed labor for him in 1863. Curtis had Levi Pease (another known Paugussett)

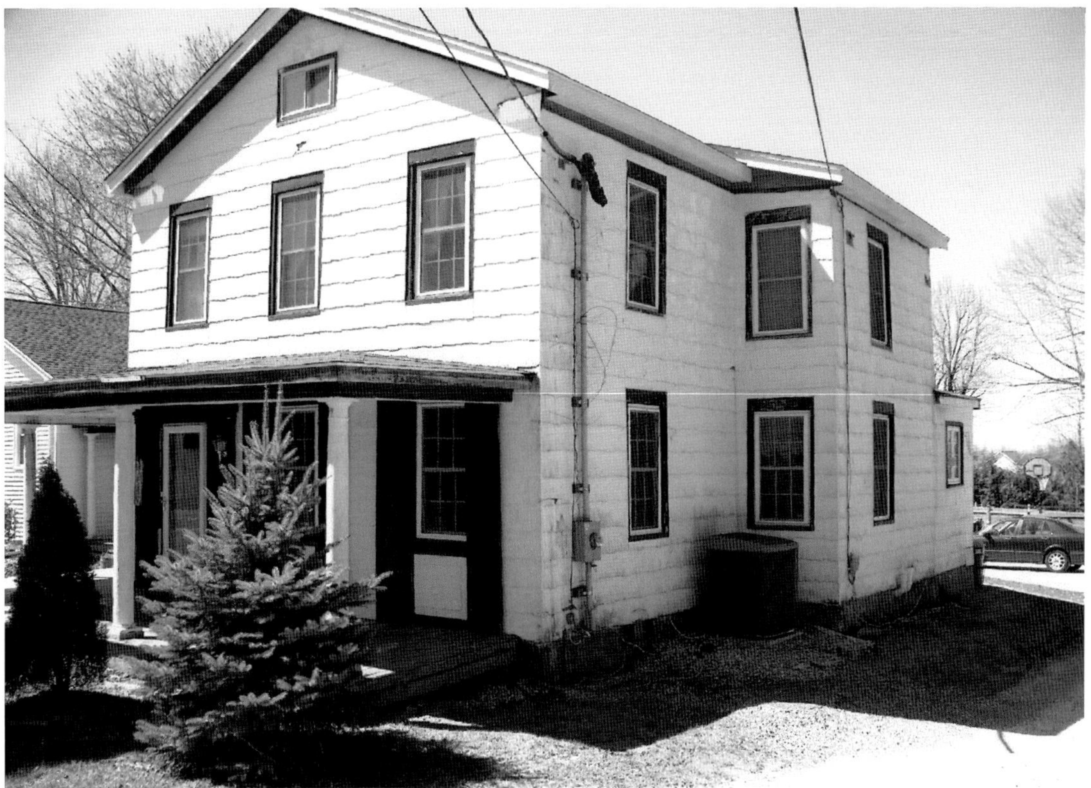

Ransom D. Curtis's 1849 homestead on Nichols Avenue, Stratford.

in his employ as a farmhand in the 1860 census. Levi died in Stratford at age sixty on December 22, 1863; Olive Pease Jackson, his niece, died there at age twenty-three on September 13, 1864; and Laura Pease, Levi's sister, died there as well at age sixty on November 24, 1865. All were known Golden Hill Paugussetts, and the cause of death listed in each instance was consumption.[175]

10.

The Dissipation of Liberia

The communities of Newfield and Waltersville, with their available low-cost building lots, had become integrated early on, especially in the aftermath of the Irish potato famine and the German political ferment of 1848. James Farm, too, had the Cooke family, white natives of England, living in the midst of the Freemans, Whites, Burrs and Martinburghs. But Liberia seems to have been a community exclusively for people of color, and to have remained so for a period of more than four decades until the urban edge of Bridgeport extended to its very border.

William Sherman, ever the taciturn New Englander in recording daily events in his journal, often wrote "went to Bridgeport," with no further explanation. He seems to specify when work was involved ("went to Bridgeport with hay for Tomson, 2 hours," January 5, 1875), or when he undertook a shopping expedition ("went to Bridgeport, bot boots," September 20, 1873). In his journal, Bridgeport also seems to be synonymous with the location of the Golden Hill Tribal Fund, as in "went to Bridgeport, got money to pay for house" (January 13, 1876), and "went to Bridgeport, got money for Henry Sherman's [Pease] family while he was in jail" (January 8, 1874). One can surmise that a simple "went to Bridgeport," with no task indicated, may have meant paying friendly calls on his kinsmen and taking part in Liberia's social whirl.

We do have evidence of the latter. William Sherman, so hardworking that he sledded logs out of the woods the day after burying his child, took a very unusual Monday off on August 4, 1873, and "went to picknick." The Bridgeport *Daily Standard* for August 5, 1873, described the Emancipation Day celebration that Sherman attended before spending the next day fishing:

> *The pic-nic of the colored people at Parlor Rock* [in Trumbull] *yesterday passed off pleasantly and peaceably...The number upon the grounds was not far from one thousand, among whom were at least a hundred white folks...The colored people returned to this city by train and carriages about 7 o'clock...where the festivities of the day were continued through the night, and did not cease until after daylight this morning.*

The onset of the "War to End Slavery" must have been greeted with exuberance in Liberia. Reverend William Serrington, a pastor of Zion Church, had come by way of the Second Street A.M.E. Zion Church in New Bedford, Massachusetts, where he had been a close associate of Frederick Douglass (it was reportedly Serrington who convinced Douglass to become ordained as a minister). Reverend Peter Ross also came to Zion Church from the same New Bedford pulpit where he also worked closely with Douglass. They were part of a string of avowed abolitionist preachers that led the church in its early decades.

The volunteers of the Twenty-ninth Colored Infantry of Connecticut organized on August 11, 1863, in New Haven. Men associated with the Liberia community who joined its ranks included George Deming, Moses H. Hayes, John Johnson Jr., Harvey Leppion, Henry Morris, Henry Parker, Henry B. Pease, George H. Purdy, Martin Storms and William VanLien (Henry Parker would be killed in action at Petersburg, Virginia, on September 1, 1864). The Thirtieth Colored Regiment (later the Thirty-first Regiment USC Infantry) included First Sergeant Thomas Douglass, Sergeant Thomas Freeman, Corporal Charles Johnson and Privates Thomas and Arthur Johnson.

Bridgeport's economy shifted into high gear during the Civil War, as immigrants from Europe as well as the rural hinterlands swelled its population (13,299 in 1860). The Duncan House Hotel never seemed to have fulfilled the expectations of its developer or his successor, and, commencing May 1, 1863, John Douglas leased "the house known by the name of the Douglas House" to Theodore Smith.[176] Other lease arrangements on record[177] give his name as Theodore Schmidt—a German. Douglas sold the hotel outright to Henry Ritzel—another German—on August 2, 1865, for $3,700.[178] The City of Bridgeport had taken title to Wolf Pit Neck just to the south that year and retained the services of Frederick Law Olmsted, Calvert Vaux and Egbert Viele—the men who had designed New York's Central Park—to create Seaside Park, the first marine rural park in America. Liberia, in the direct path of development in the postwar era, would never again be an insular, self-contained entity far on the outskirts of town.

The German hotel operators were almost certainly attracted to the vicinity by the expansion of the Furniture Manufacturing Company, run by their countryman, Jacob Kiefer. His company had been organized in 1852 to make household furnishings with the aid of machinery. By the time of the Civil War it had relocated to the shores of Bridgeport Harbor immediately to the north of Liberia, and was soon to become the largest furniture-making business in the eastern United States.[179] Between 1870 and 1873, Russell Tomlinson (coincidentally Golden Hill tribal overseer at the time) participated in the construction of blocks of workers' tenements between Main and Broad Streets between the modest homes of Liberia and the railroad tracks. These buildings became occupied by mostly German tenants.

Mary Freeman, as previously noted, had sold her brother Joel's four houses to the Naugatuck Railroad Company in 1870 ("said grantor is to have the right to select and remove one of the houses now on said land and to use the same for a wood house or out house only, the other buildings are to be torn down by said grantee and said grantor is to have the old materials by removing same"), which filled in a portion of the harbor to extend its dock and construct a freight yard. The *Bridgeport Standard* described the process:[180]

> *One of the greatest improvements of the age is the long dock, building by the Naugatuck R.R. Co. About one hundred workmen are employed, and it is rapidly approaching completion. The great "Behemoth" that is "gobbling up" all the mud in the vicinity, is attracting the profound attention of the "dock committee," and some of them stand for hours and watch the "opening and shutting" of its "ponderous jaws"—it works "like a thing of life." It dives down with mouth wide open; closes its jaws upon any thing that comes in its way; rises, opens its mouth, showing its big teeth, and vomits forth mud, clams, stones, &c., into large scows; and goes on repeating its evolutions at the will of man, and to the great curiosity of a large number of lookers on.*

There was talk of the Singer Sewing Machine Company relocating to more of Liberia's acres in 1870 (Singer Avenue was so named in anticipation), but the company was to remain in New Jersey until its merger with the Bridgeport firm of Wheeler & Wilson in 1906.

In 1876, Doctors I. DeVer and Lucien C. Warner (the Warner Brothers) were attracted to Bridgeport and began operations manufacturing their patented "health corsets" in a new facility one block to the west of Liberia. The plant doubled in size in 1878 and again in 1880, and by 1881 Warner Brothers was the largest manufacturer of corsets in the world, with a workforce of one thousand. On June 23, 1883, the *Bridgeport Standard* reported:

> *Very few people have a correct idea of the rapid improvement of the southern part of the city and of the numerous buildings now in progress below the railroad between Broad Street and Park Avenue, there being over fifty houses by actual count now in process of construction in that portion, all of which are of a good class, well built and designed, and very generally are replete with all modern improvements.*

Among the fifty or so houses were three dozen Victorian Gothic workers' houses built between Main and Broad Streets by the president of the New Haven Railroad.[181] Seemingly an early example of urban redevelopment, this project resulted in the destruction of a number of old houses in the heart of Liberia. The new dwellings were rented exclusively to whites.

Seaside Park, meanwhile, attracted the interest of wealthy businessmen and industrialists who began building palatial homes around its periphery. P.T. Barnum led the way with the construction of his mansion Waldemere in 1868, and by the late nineteenth century this part of the South End was known as "Bridgeport's Faubourg St. Germain."[182]

Like the old Indians in the seventeenth century, the inhabitants of Liberia tried for a time to cling to the ways they knew and the old community that had been their home in the face of disorienting urbanization. The inauguration of the Bridgeport

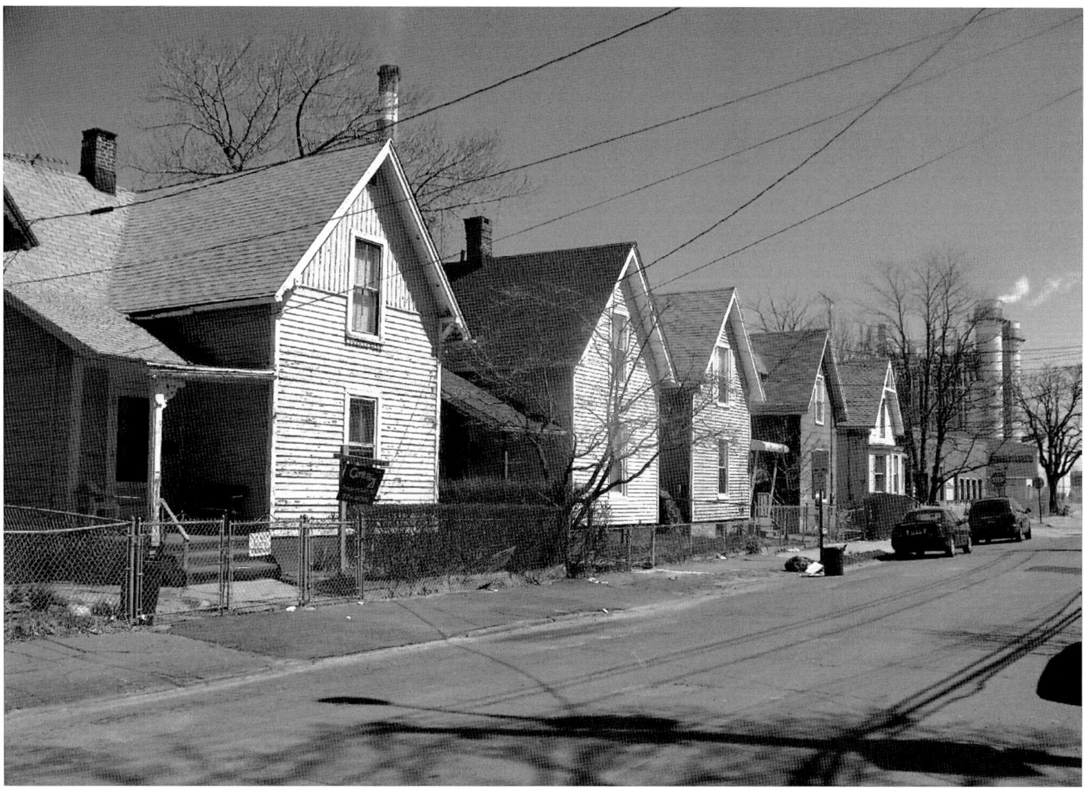

William D. Bishop's cottage development of 1880, Atlantic Street.

Steamboat Company in 1865 brought new employment possibilities, and "steamboat cook" and "steamboat waiter" replaced "seaman" as the most frequent employment of community residents in post-Civil War census records.

The Strengthening of Community Institutions

Zion Church undertook the construction of a new edifice in 1882. Of Queen Anne/ Eastlake design, it was probably designed by the architectural firm of Palliser, Palliser and Company, a firm with a national reputation that was responsible for much of the new appearance of the South End. The *Bridgeport Standard* of October 23, 1882, described the dedication:

> *The new edifice of the A.M.E. Zion Church having been completed was formally dedicated yesterday afternoon with appropriate services. About every available space in the body of the church was filled and many could not gain access to the building. Among the audience were many of our prominent citizens and a large delegation from the neighboring towns...At the close of the sermon Rev. R.G.S. McNeille was appointed collector. He*

remarked upon the efforts and struggles of the colored people during the past two or three years to provide for themselves a suitable place of worship and their success in erecting the present edifice...Mr. [P.T.] *Barnum spoke substantially as follows: "I subscribed and paid $100—to day I have added $25. Now these poor people will have hard work to support their church after all its debts are paid. I will, therefore, pay one-twelfth part of the remainder of the debt, about $2,600, provided the other eleven-twelfths are subscribed by our citizens within six months. I am considered a heretic by some, and hope that the Christians, heretics, and all others will raise the balance of the debt. My heresy teaches that faith and hope are as tinkling cymbals unless they are founded on the greatest Christian principle—charity"...A handsome silver communion set was presented to the church by Colonel James D. Frary, and a handsome silver water pitcher was given them by the waiters at the Atlantic hotel. Both of these gifts are highly appreciated by the church people.*

It should be remembered that Presence Jackson, live-in servant to P.T. Barnum, had been landlady to the Zion Church pastor a quarter-century previous; Presence's daughter, Ellen Deming, was secretary of the Daughters of Zion, an organization that provided some financing for the new church. Barnum was a major stockholder in the Bridgeport Steamboat Company, employer of a significant portion of the Zion Church congregation.

Liberia continued to grow and develop through the late nineteenth century. On September 21, 1871, community members organized Doric Lodge 4, Free and Accepted Masons (Prince Hall). Officers listed in the 1871–72 *City Directory* [183] are, "W.M., Uriah W. Pelham; S.W., Frank M. Welch; J.W., Edwin Freeman; Sec., George T. Barclay; Treas., Garrison Murray; S.D., Henry Hawley; J.D., W.H. Brown" (According to Orcutt, Edwin Freeman, George of the James Farm community's brother, was the only veteran of the Twenty-ninth or Thirtieth Regiments to be listed as a member of Bridgeport's Elias Howe Post, G.A.R., in 1886).

Doric Lodge was more than a mere social club. A newspaper account of the 1873 Emancipation Day picnic at a grove outside the city[184] illustrates the protective role the organization played in the Bridgeport community:

No liquors were sold upon the grounds, and the officers of the Doric Lodge and of the Welch Guard did all in their power to prevent the sale of liquor outside. Nevertheless there were quantities of it sold, and a few little friendly fights were the result. James Burgess and a colored man established a booth for selling liquor just outside of the pic-nic grounds. They had no license from the town of Trumbull, and as that town had voted to grant no licenses, they were forbidden to sell by the proprietor of the grounds, Mr. Royal Jennings. They defied him and continued the traffic. The Good Templars of the place then took the matter up, and tried to get an injunction served upon them, but of all the grand jurors chosen at the last election none had been qualified, and it was necessary to get an ex-grand juror to sign the document. It was then found that the only constable who had qualified was out of town. The Worthy Chief Templar was deputized to act in that capacity, and he with others tried to arrest Burgess, but the crowd pitched into them and took the prisoners away. We learn

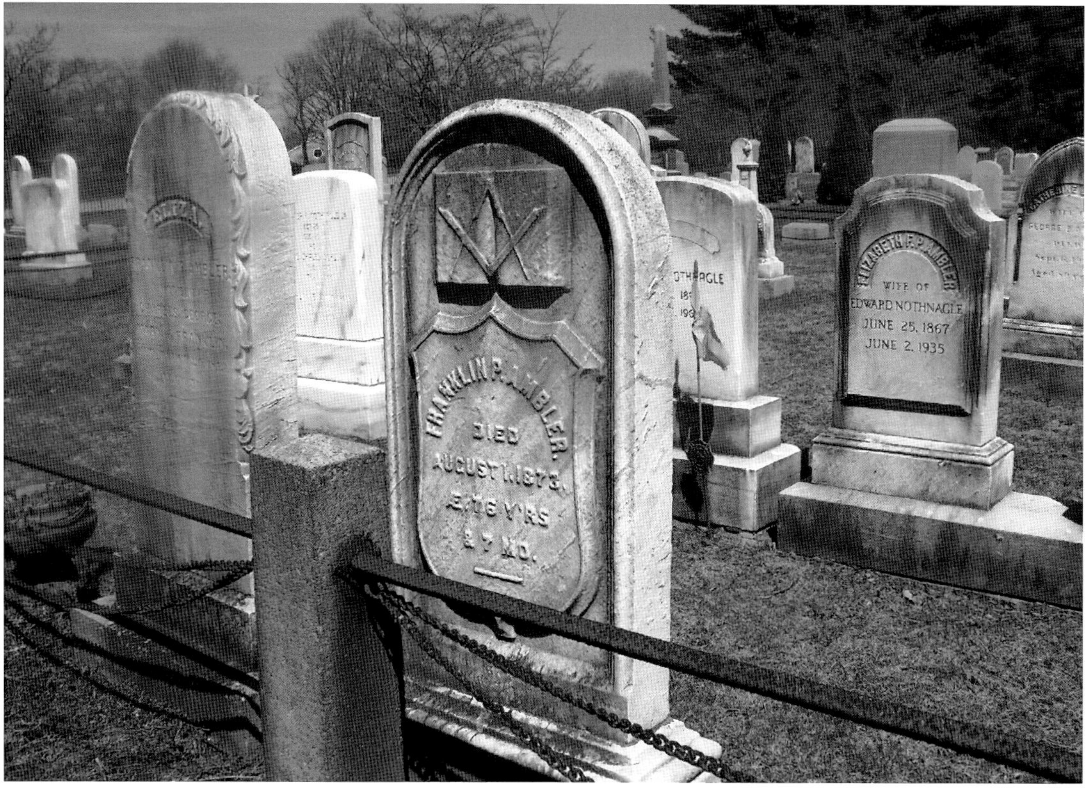

Franklin Ambler's grave, dug by his faithful friend William Sherman.

> *that a warrant for the arrest of Burgess has since been issued by the town of Trumbull... The officers of Doric Lodge, and of the Welch Guard regret that on account of the action of outsiders in selling liquor, many of those who attended the pic-nic and the ball should have disgraced themselves by intoxication and fighting.*

It should be noted that Franklin Ambler, one of the highest-ranking members of the Masonic fraternity in the Bridgeport area, had been buried two days previous. The *Daily Standard* noted, "A large number of Masons were present and he was buried with Masonic ceremonies. The delegation of friends from this city [Bridgeport] was very large."

A Cohesive Community No Longer

Paugussett descendants from backcountry Connecticut continued to move to Bridgeport and take their places in this community (Bridgeport's population grew to 19,876 in 1870 and 29,153 in 1880). Joseph B. Morris[185] and his wife, Chloe Brush Sherman Morris, came from Brookfield and first appear in the Bridgeport *City Directory* for 1877 at 15 Gregory Street (the former John Elsey property). They

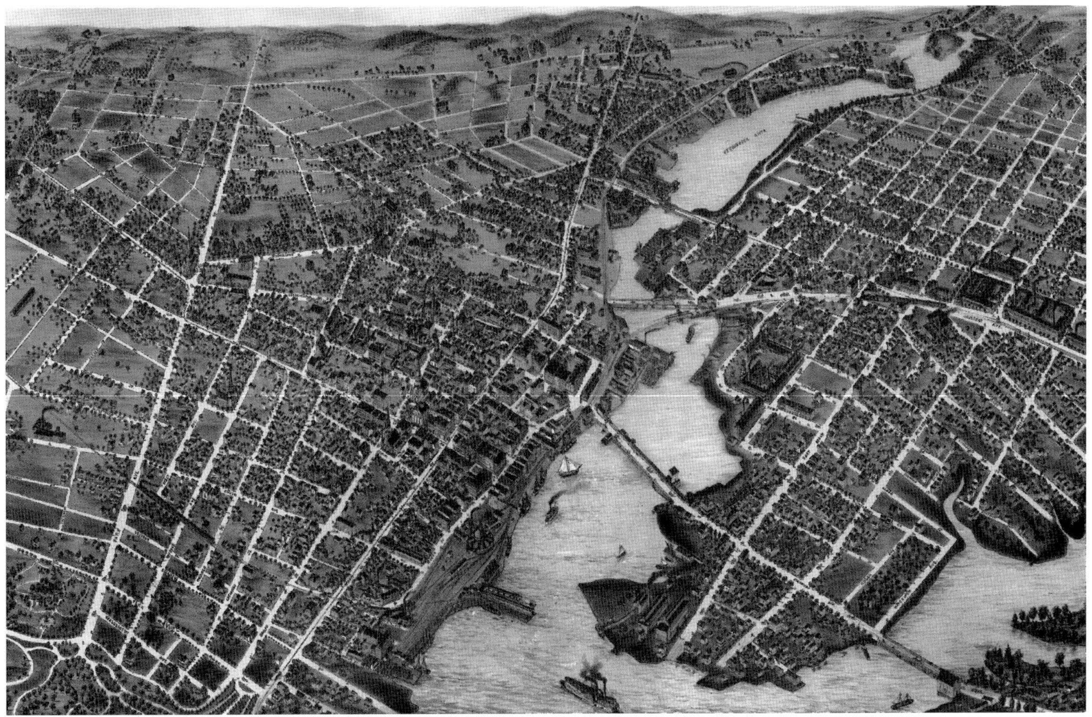

Bridgeport was turning into a bona fide city by 1875.

shared this house with Charles H. Thompson, and both Thompson and Morris worked as waiters at the Atlantic Hotel in downtown Bridgeport (the waiters at that hostelry, as noted earlier, would donate a silver water pitcher at the dedication of Zion Church's new edifice). Thompson reportedly kept a diary of his activities in the 1870s, and there is a recollection in his family of Native American descent.[186] The 1881 *City Directory* lists John A. DeWillis (husband of Mary Francis Sherman, Chloe's sister) as residing across the street at 18 Gregory Street—a house owned by Mary Freeman—and also working as a waiter at the Atlantic Hotel. The proprietor of this establishment at the time was Peter Foland, former proprietor of the Nelson House in Poughkeepsie, New York.[187] DeWillis's son Richard appears first in the 1902 *City Directory* at 30 Whiting Street, previously the home of Eliza Hayes. He is the tenant of Mrs. Georgia Brewster (nee Georgiana Hubbard), originally of Norwich,[188] who was thought to be a Nehantic woman from a family originally named Waukeet.

But Bridgeport's Native American community did become less cohesive as the nineteenth century wore on. A flood of new African American immigrants arrived from the Southern states, and better housing opportunities became available. Areas such as Elm Street and the Wales Block on Main Street opened up to people of color, and the Newfield community expanded significantly. Other community residents moved to Naugatuck Valley towns like Derby and Ansonia, including William Sherman Jr., recorded as "removed to Birmingham" (Derby) in the 1891 *City Directory*. Liberia, meanwhile, became part of an inner city industrial district, and its aging housing stock became a low-rent district for the multitude of immigrants pouring into Bridgeport (1890 population of 43,866). The 1895 *City Directory* (the first to be cross-referenced by address) shows Whiting Street populated by individuals with names like Patrick Flynn, carman; Michael Shanley, saloonkeeper; August Doerr, employed Burns, Silver & Co.; and Rocco Fabrizio, shoemaker. Over on Main Street, the Reverend Collins's grocery store of 1855 had been subdivided to provide quarters for two businesses: Jacob Goldstein, shoemaker and—as if to underscore how things had changed from the time when almost every woman in the Liberia community was employed as a laundress—Sing Lee, laundry.

11.

William Sherman and the Land Base

We know that William Sherman lived the life of a sailor for seventeen years, according to Richard Ambler's contribution to Orcutt's *History of Stratford and Bridgeport*. This would account for the period of his life from approximately 1840 (aged fifteen) until the time his son William was born in Trumbull (and his first dated "a count" with overseer Dwight Morris was made) in 1857. Rensselaer Pease had died in April of 1856, and family responsibilities may have prevented William from returning to sea.

William had also tried city life in Bridgeport, and he may well have had a role in Rensselaer's boat building business. But William instead opted for the life of a countryman, and he made a decision to live in the bucolic community of Nichols Farms, an easy horseback ride from the city but surrounded by woods and fields and in proximity to the Housatonic River, traditional life spring of the Paugussett people.

Evidence seems to show that William grew up in Rensselaer Pease's household. Rensselaer had acquired a small landholding in the town of Monroe, just to the north of Trumbull, shortly after William's birth. Reuben Cam, later Rensselaer's shipbuilding partner, was also in Monroe at this time. This homestead may have been the setting for William's education in the rural arts: the logging, butchering, cider making, basket weaving and "dockterin" (presumably with traditional Indian herbal medicines) of which we have record.

The Wells Hollow Turnpike farm, established for the tribe at Nichols Farms when William was sixteen, also seems to have played an important role in his life, even if it was only as a concept contemplated from the vantage point of a whaling ship in distant seas. The land base at Golden Hill, lost to the tribe twenty-three years before his birth, had been reestablished, and the possibility of preserving tribal culture and heritage away from the corrupting influence of the city must have been of more than passing interest to all members of the Paugussett fraternity.

But as we have already seen, this land was taken from the tribe the year following William's marriage. We do know that Levi and Laura Pease, Rensselaer's siblings; Olive Pease Jackson, his daughter; and members of the Pan family remained close

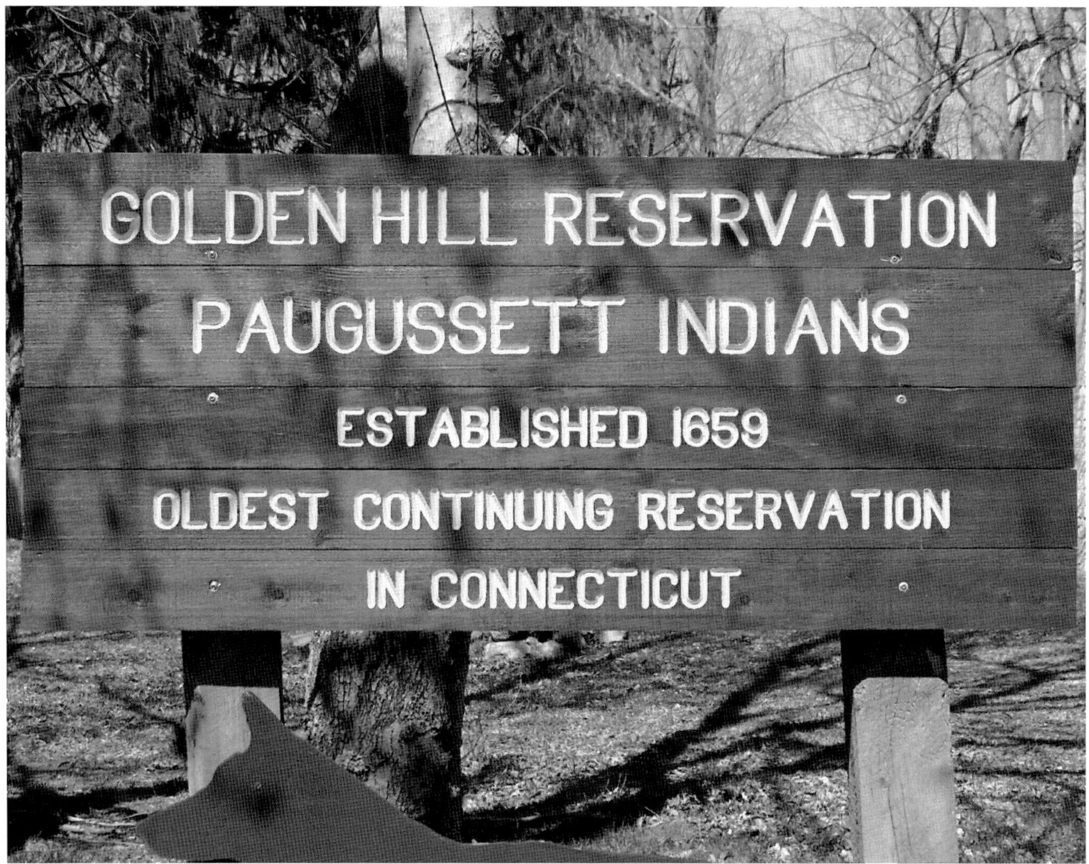

William Sherman's lasting legacy on Shelton Road, Trumbull.

to Nichols Farms, mostly employed as farmhands. Hurd's description of the ancient stone-walled spring being uncovered in the village, presumably another Richard Ambler contribution, says "it was unknown to the descendants of Golden Hill Indians living in the vicinity," revealing that they formed a community that could be consulted regarding cultural memory.

At the age of fifty,[189] William paid fifty dollars for a quarter-acre lot with some sort of shack already standing on it[190] directly across the road from the site of the 1841–54 farmstead. This transaction took place soon after the death of "the Old Man" Franklin Ambler, William's patron and mentor (the grantor was Franklin's son Charles). He set about immediately constructing a proper two-and-a-half-story house, in no way inferior in size, style or finish to its contemporaries elsewhere in Nichols Farms village. The Golden Hill Tribal Fund loaned him $800 (he was not considered indigent) for construction costs.[191] We know from the quality of this structure (it stood for a century) that William Sherman must have been looking beyond the comforts of his old age to his posterity.

By the 1880s it would have been obvious to William that the tribal community that had survived in Bridgeport for more than a half century was under cultural assault on all sides. The founders of Ethiope had mostly passed from the scene (Mary Freeman was one of the last in 1883), and a new generation was becoming numerically engulfed by the mass of new migrants from the South. The tight bonds that had held the community together were slowly dissolving, and Sherman may have looked with consternation on the materialism of city life and the turning away from the old ways.

William appears to have taken it upon himself to restore, if only in some token manner, the land base of the Paugussett tribe. He took the necessary steps during the last few months of his life, giving up title to his hard-earned property and the house built with his own sweat and toil for the good of his people.[192]

12.

William Sherman's Aftermath

Newspapers of the 1840s had been rife with stories of massacres of whites during the Seminole War in Florida; other sundry items depicted Native Americans as fearsome sideshow attractions. This may account for the Paugussetts of that day being understandably reticent about trumpeting their Indian identity to the public at large—it had, after all, been only a few years since the townspeople of Derby had torched Native wigwams and exiled the survivors of a terrible epidemic outside the municipal limits.

Three decades after Longfellow published his "Song of Hiawatha" and a decade following Little Big Horn, however, sophisticated Easterners in rising urban centers like Bridgeport tended to embrace Native Americans as "Noble Savages." They collected Indian handicrafts, eagerly purchased patent medicines purported to be secret ancient tribal formulations and took an avid interest in archeological findings (excavations at the "Indian Lot," site of the 1765–1802 reservation, were undertaken as early as the 1850s).[193]

It is in this context that William Sherman emerges as the first of the Paugussett Indian celebrities at the close of his life. He achieved widespread notoriety from his likeness and lineage and was a prominent component of Orcutt's *History of Stratford and Bridgeport*. Bridgeport people became conscious of the tribe surviving in their midst and fascinated by the "romance" of its history.[194]

When William Sherman died on May 18, 1886, he was accorded an obituary equal to that which would have been written for a prominent banker, industrialist or businessman, and certainly not one typical of a farm and turnpike laborer. The United States Census for Trumbull lists Sherman as an Indian in 1880, as does his Trumbull death record. Similarly, death records in the city of Ansonia during the decades of the 1880s and '90s show members of the Phillips family to have been recorded as Indians.

The Golden Hill tribe became fodder for Sunday newspaper reporters throughout the twentieth century. First, George Sherman, William's son, was depicted in a feathered

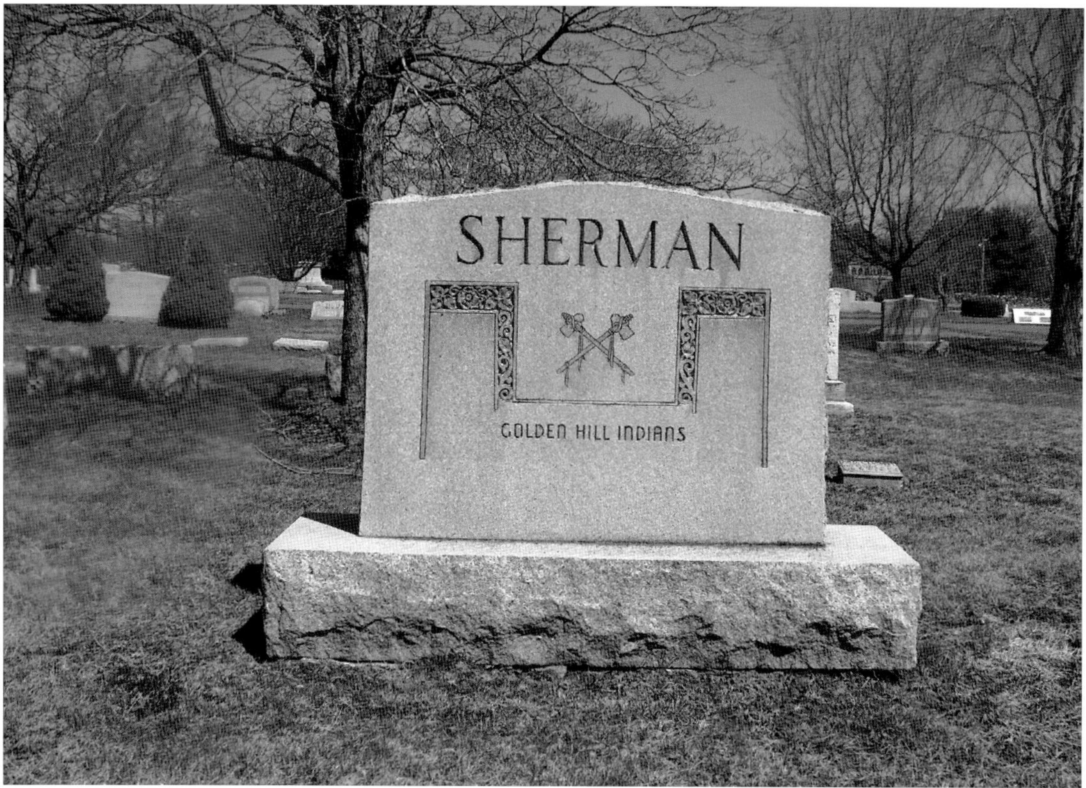

William Sherman's grave marker on his burial plot, Nichols Farms Cemetery.

war bonnet, tomahawk in hand, speaking about his special rights vis-à-vis hunting and fishing rights and his exemption from town property taxes and dog licensing fees. Years later, his son Edward gave much the same interview and photographic poses. They were always labeled "the last of their tribe."

William's granddaughter Ethel became an important force in tribal affairs. She had made a fortune in real estate (in the tradition of Paugussett women such as Mary and Eliza Freeman) and had been particularly interested in a development called Laurel Park along Chopsey Hill Road and Agnes and May Streets in North Bridgeport, where she held title to twenty-three lots.[195] Her visits to tribal members in Bridgeport and the hard-pressed towns of the Lower Naugatuck Valley to provide moral and financial assistance during the Great Depression are still recalled. An advertisement she placed in the *Bridgeport Post* on February 24, 1934, gives us some insight into her activities at that time:

> *INDIAN TRADING POST—Lost relatives and articles found by "Chieftess Rising Star." Your past, present, and future by the only full blooded Indian in Conn. Council Gathering every Monday and Friday evening at 8 p.m. 425 Harrall Avenue. Sitting Bull's grandson will open the meeting Mon.*

Ethel took her leadership role most seriously and was often in the pages of the newspaper, asserting her rights as a Native American in interviews and in her own spirited letters to the editor. She also corresponded with state and national leaders—including the president—on behalf of her people.

The story of the occupants of the Golden Hill Reservation was well known to the people of the Greater Bridgeport area through widespread publicity in the century following William Sherman's purchase of the quarter-acre. Then, in the 1970s, it became a recurrent feature in the national media.

But, again, this was not the whole story of the tribe.

Due to its limited capacity, the reservation was capable of housing only one family. The remainder of the tribe was to survive through the twentieth century in three communities: Bridgeport, Ansonia and the rural sector.

As we have seen, the tightknit residential enclave of Liberia dispersed over time to other areas of Bridgeport (the city's population had mushroomed from 70,996 in 1900 to 173,000 in 1917), but the Indian community remained centered on Zion Church[196] and other institutions such as the Masonic lodge. Walters Memorial historian Mary L. McDuffie, from interviews with elderly church members, stated, "It was common knowledge that Indians were an important part of our congregation during the 20th century."[197] Belle Fuller Pease, for example, remained in Liberia at 415 Main Street (diagonally opposite Mary Freeman's former residence) until her death in 1944. Chloe Brush Sherman and her husband Joseph Morris moved out to the Newfield district to 131 Beardsley Street. Their daughter Grace May (married to George Toran) lived a block away at 57 Smith Street until her death in 1949. Today a substantial portion of the tribe's membership resides within the corporate limits of Bridgeport.

The Tinney family and their descendants are the second important component of the surviving Paugussett tribe. They resided consistently in the Fourth Ward of the city of Ansonia for many years, fifteen miles to the northeast of Bridgeport, and their community was centered on the Clinton A.M.E Zion Church. The Tinneys and their antecedents, the Allens and Phillipses, were long credited in local histories and newspaper accounts with being Native Americans and descendants of the Paugussett tribe. A relative of the Bridgeport Deming clan married into their ranks early in the twentieth century.

A community existed here along Factory Street and its immediate environs in the mid–twentieth century that was populated by Tinneys as well as Sherman descendants from the Trumbull reservation. All were related through native bloodlines (in the words of Chief Quiet Hawk, who grew up on Factory Street, "In a small town like Ansonia with a limited minority population, every member of the extended family was a cousin two or three times over"—exactly the situation that seems to have prevailed at Liberia a century previous). To the present day, all are quite conscious of their Indian identity and of their relationship with tribal members in the other communities.

While agriculture survived as a way of life in Fairfield County, Native American families remained scattered across the countryside. For example, John Benson, son of the Civil War veteran buried in George Freeman's cemetery plot, was a noted Indian basket maker on the outskirts of Derby through the 1940s. Rob Starr, a farm laborer in the towns of Huntington and Monroe, also survived into the 1940s, as did the Cam family in Shelton. All of these people were written up in their respective town histories as proud descendants of the Golden Hill Paugussett tribe.

13.

Filling in the Blanks— Tribal Leadership and Continuity

As we have seen, a significant majority of the Paugussett tribe's membership probably took heed of the lessons imparted during the time of great upheaval in the seventeenth and early eighteenth centuries and fled to inland sanctuaries. The concentration camp-like conditions described in the early years of the Golden Hill Reservation—one hundred wigwams crowded onto eighty acres of mostly rock outcrop—certainly contributed to the decision of many to opt out. Traditional tribal summer gatherings at the shore are described through the end of the seventeenth century, after which accounts cease. The white population was exploding and advancing year by year into the wooded hills of interior Connecticut, driving the native population before them. The late seventeenth and the eighteenth centuries would see effort after effort by the Indians to regroup and make a stand in the face of white onslaught. Almost all were doomed to failure.

Paugussetts were almost surely among the one thousand Algonquin refugees who settled at Schaghticoke in the aftermath of King Phillip's War (1675–76). Others came to dwell with their Mahican kinsmen in the Taconic Mountain region of Putnam, Dutchess and Columbia Counties in New York or along the Housatonic River in western Massachusetts. These latter survivors were mostly gathered into a mission in the town of Stockbridge in the year 1730 and were afterward known as the Stockbridge Indians. Still other Paugussett may have moved in with the Oneida at Marshall, New York, to form a community that was known as Brothertown. In later years, this group would remove yet again to Wisconsin. Similar amalgamated communities that may have incorporated Paugussett tribe remnants eventually ended up in Oklahoma and Ontario, Canada.

Yet, in common with some other tribes of the northeast, there were a fair number of Paugussett families who elected not to join the great migration to the north and west and to stray from the scenes of their youth. These families, scattered across western Connecticut and eastern New York, gradually became Christians over the course of the eighteenth century. By the time of the American Revolution, they had for the most part adopted the English language and the Anglo-Saxon surnames of their white neighbors, dressed in the European manner and lived in frame houses rather than traditional wigwams. They adapted to the trappings of the dominant culture as a means of survival, preserving their Native American culture and contacts away from the eyes of the white population.

The best documented of these families that remained is the Shoron, later known as the Sherman family. They were the very last to occupy the reservation at Golden Hill, and oral tradition holds them as the "keepers" of this place that was long held sacred by the tribe. Golden Hill itself is an eminence that rises some eighty feet above the surrounding plain. As the hill was built upon by whites over the course of the nineteenth century, it was found to be almost entirely covered with native burials, attesting to its significance as a sacred site. The *Bridgeport Standard* of October 28, 1870, stated, "The frequent finding of Indian bones and skulls...suggests the question whether Bridgeport may not have been at some remote period in the past one immense Indian hunting and burying ground. Every few days these bones are being brought to light by excavations." When the Town of Bridgeport laid out Elm Street at the base of the hill in 1827, it was constructed over a layer of clam and oyster shells many feet deep, indicating a lengthy occupancy by the Paugussett tribe. Until 1802, when the tribe's removal was forced, Golden Hill remained the place of residence of the sachem and his family.

Sachem Tom Sherman died in 1801 and is known to have been succeeded by his son Tom Jr. (1753–1849). The younger Sherman presided over one of the darkest periods of Paugussett history, when the land base was entirely extinguished and the tribe all but overwhelmed by an expansionist white society. The woodlands and wild rivers that had sustained the tribe for centuries were disappearing under exploitative circumstances. It is estimated that by 1820, 80 percent of Connecticut's forests had been cleared for use by agriculture, and that nearly all streams with suitable water power had been impounded for use by industry. The tribe was forced to adapt or perish.

The Early Nineteenth Century

The first decades of the nineteenth century are perhaps the murkiest in discerning the tribe's activities. All of the Paugussetts were residing "off-reservation" at this point. Most towns did not begin the compilation of vital records prior to the 1830s; census takers recorded only the names of male heads of households; and town historians generally ended their chapters on the history of the Indians with the period of the 1760s. Nevertheless, the sporadic records that remain, and later developments that grew out of this period, indicate that the tribe most certainly maintained community and that the membership remained very much in contact.

A handful of families attempted to continue life in a more or less traditional manner. We have a number of testimonies of the Pan family weaving split-ash baskets at their inland campsites and making periodic journeys to the coastal towns of Bridgeport, Stratford and Fairfield to peddle their wares and seek itinerant work as farm laborers. One account makes note of their annual campsite in Bridgeport above Old Mill

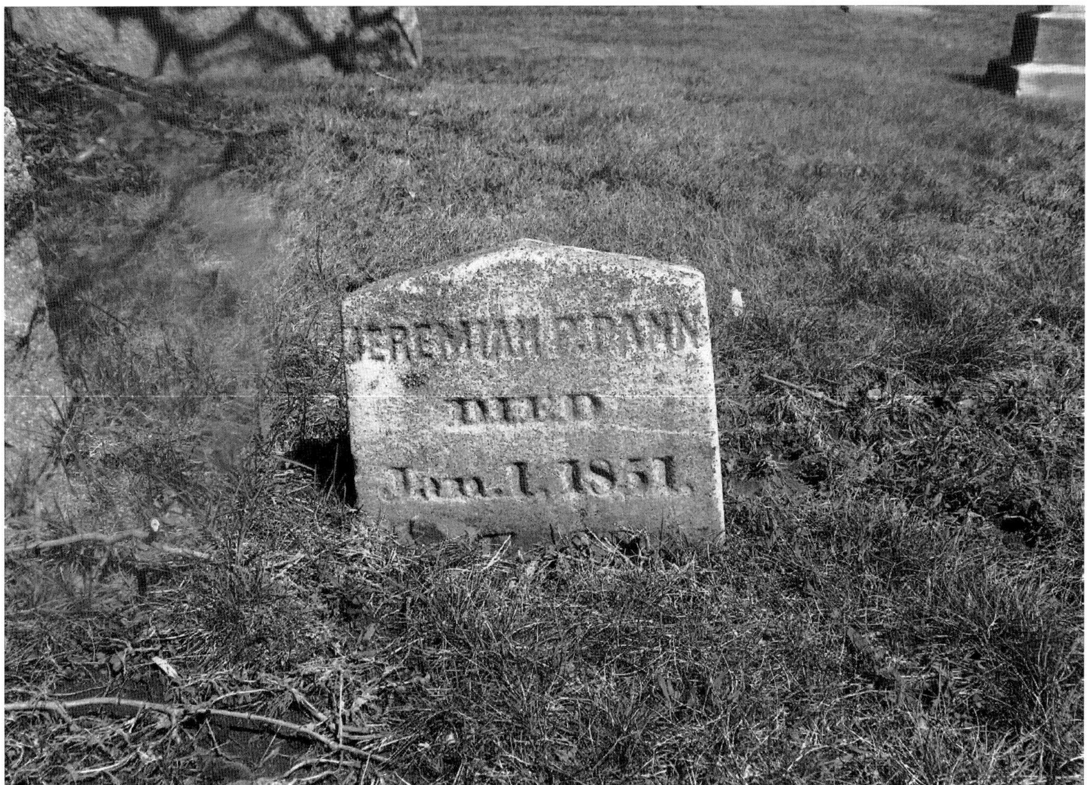

Jerry Pan's grave marker on William Sherman's burial plot, Nichols Farms Cemetery.

Green, a site where Nob Hill Apartment construction a century later (1953) found evidence of the location of a major pre-contact village. This family's traditional lifestyle continued until the death of Jerry Pan in 1851. In the hills above Derby, we know that the Macks and their kin were living in traditional bark wigwams through the time of the smallpox epidemic of 1833. Their neighbors and fellow Paugussetts the Freemans/Hulls, however, resided on an adjoining parcel that was known as the "Rock House Lot," probably indicating that they had adapted European building practices and presumably other acculturations as well.

The late John P. Menta's treatise on a neighboring tribe, the Quinnipiac, documents annual visits by members of that dispersed group to shoreline sites for purposes of fish and shellfish procurement through the 1840s. Similarly, we have records of members of the Paugussett tribe visiting their traditional coastal haunts during this same period. We know they made the annual trek to what was known as Walker's Beach on the Johnson Farm, today the place where Newfield Avenue meets the harbor in Bridgeport's East End. There is a story related in several Stratford town histories of Indians journeying from inland towns and occupying an abandoned farmhouse for purposes of harvesting turtles from the Housatonic estuary. This practice appears to have ceased after local youths torched the dwelling—while the Indians were in occupancy—during the summer of 1840.

But by and large, the survivors of the Paugussett tribe appear to have settled into an accommodation with white society during the first years of the nineteenth century. Many of them appear to have lived as research indicates Agrippa Pease and Amos Freeman did, which would mean they purchased a small holding of an acre or two and erected a rudimentary frame shack, usually valued at less than fifty dollars. They retained their traditional skills (herbal medicine, basket making, etc.) while honing some marketable skills in the mainstream economy (carpentry, masonry, orchard and farm work). They lost their native language, joined mainstream church societies and outwardly differed from their Anglo-Saxon neighbors primarily in the color of their skin. Yet from their marriage patterns alone it is obvious that they remained very much aware of their Paugussett identity and shared heritage.

Just who were these survivors of the Paugussett Indian nation? Nineteenth-century public records are helpful mainly with regard to members of the Sherman clan, who had an ongoing relationship with the State of Connecticut and its appointed overseers. Certain others (Jacksons, Freemans, Macks, Peases, Phillipses, Moses, Cams, Starrs) are signatories to deeds dispersing Indian lands, or are credited as being Indians in certain town histories. Knowledge of other members of the Paugussett tribe requires further digging. For example, Henry O. and Jeanette Pease had a seven-month-old son who died of bronchitis on October 17, 1883. His death record in the vital records of Stratford[198] gives the race of both parents as Indian. Census records prior to 1870, it should be remembered, list tribal members variously as colored, black or white.

It is from marriage and residence patterns, then, that we can primarily deduce the membership of the Paugussett tribe in the early nineteenth century. The Simons/Simonds family of Southbury, for example, consistently married members of known Paugussett families. They appear to have made a collective decision to move en masse to the Bridgeport Indian settlement by the 1840s, abandoning their rural home. At about the same time, the Deming family of Southbury, Woodbury and Middlebury (towns which adjoin one another) similarly moved to that city. They intermarried with the Paugussett Jacksons as well as the Shinnecock Bloom family.

Members of the Edwards clan of Newtown (which adjoins Southbury to the west) were labeled Native Americans in marriage and other records, which have been found. They played an important role in the development of the Bridgeport community, as financiers as well as marriage partners of important personages in the village hierarchy. The women of the Gibson family of Southbury and Newtown (a single family that moved between both municipalities) tie together in marriage Rensselaer Pease, Philander Pitts and Simeon Dickson. Their brother Joshua became the first minister of the Bridgeport church. The Brush family daughters, also Newtown residents, married Rensselaer Pease's father Agrippa and Tunis Green, pioneer member of the Bridgeport settlement. The Sauls/Sills family, the Hawleys (of Trumbull), the Purdys, Hubbells and others all have knowledge of Paugussett heritage, marriage and residence patterns that seem to prove the contention.

The Paugussett Revival

Had the Paugussetts continued to live in isolated rural localities, it is likely that the bonds that had held the tribe together from contact times could have disintegrated and the tribal community completely amalgamated into mainstream society. As it turned out, however, the tribe came together and formed a new community, based on shared work in the growing seaport town of Bridgeport and the common interests of the gathering membership. They formed a Paugussett village, segregated from the white town a half-mile to the north, with its own society and social institutions. The new village kept the tribe going during a critical period when other tribes of southern New England faded into oblivion.

The impetus behind the formation of the Bridgeport community is not clear from a distance of almost two centuries and a complete lack of interest on the part of nineteenth-century Bridgeport historians. What we do know is that Jacob Freeman, a member of the Freeman/Phillips clan of Derby/Orange/Milford, bought a house near Bridgeport's lower harbor in 1821 in partnership with John Feeley, who appears to be his brother-in-law. Four years later Jacob's brother, Benjamin, came from North Stratford (a neighbor and likely kin of another Paugussett clan of Freemans) and built a house to the south of his sibling. After another four years, Benjamin's daughter Rosanna and her husband built the third house in the community, this one directly on the harbor front. The following year, Philip Freeman established his homestead immediately to the south of Benjamin. And then a year later (1831), Joel Freeman came from Derby and moved a building to a lot next to Rosanna and established his residence at a point of land between a salt creek and the wide mouth of Bridgeport Harbor.

Thus for a decade the community in the South End of Bridgeport remained a virtual fiefdom of the Freeman family. Joel Freeman exhibited all the traits of a village chieftain (sagamore) in what we are able to glean from public records—witness to secured loans, witness to marriages of likely tribal members, executor of estates of deceased community members, founding trustee of a church and petitioner to the Connecticut General Assembly for funds to support a school that had already been established by the inhabitants of the village. He was able to read and write and was probably instrumental in easing the transition into urban life of those who were unfamiliar with the rudiments of functioning in the white man's society.

It should be remembered that Tom Sherman Jr., who was approaching his eightieth birthday, remained titular head of the Paugussett tribe. He resided in Trumbull during his last years and appears to have left the responsibility for the growing Bridgeport community under Joel's aegis.

In 1833 another of the great Paugussett clans made its appearance in the South End. The Jacksons—in the person of Presence Jackson, married to a man named Henry Cooke (likely Mahican from the Hudson Valley)—purchased a home, the first to be built on Main Street. They were soon joined by the Demings, with whom they became tied by the marriage of their daughter. To the south of this household, Tunis Green (brother-in-law of Agrippa Pease) secured a homestead the following year.

The next year, 1835, saw the founding of Zion Church, lodestone of the new village and its focal point for many decades to come. Over the next few years Whiting Street was developed as family after family left the backcountry and sought the community of their fellow tribesmen and the possibilities of participation in an urban economy. There were a number of African Americans who also gravitated to the village, in a majority of instances that can be discerned the spouses of Paugussett women.

The year 1841 saw the arrival of Simeon Dickson, who is known to have been a missionary to the Eastern Pequot tribe, and his brother-in-law Philander Pitts (their wives were nieces of Rensselaer Pease). It was at exactly this time that the petition was launched to garner funding from the state school fund for the educational institution that the village had been attempting to operate without public assistance. Shortly afterward, the church body underwent a schism, with the majority of the congregation (Indian) pulling out and leaving the small minority (African American) with the existing building and constructing a new edifice a short distance to the north—an extraordinary measure to "purify" the institution and emphasize the Native American form of worship. As stated earlier, the tablet over the door of the newer structure reads, "The Glory of the Latter House Shall Exceed That of the Former," in what almost appears to be a nose-thumbing gesture.

The year of 1841 was an important time in the rural community as well. Eunice Sherman, who is thought to have played a role in the tribal hierarchy complementary to her brother as "squaw sachem," died; William Sherman shipped out for the first time on a whaling vessel; and the State of Connecticut allocated monies from the Golden Hill Tribal Fund to purchase land for a new reservation.

Chief Tom Sherman, who had been born in a distant time when the tribe still had possession of the full eighty acres of the Golden Hill Reservation in Bridgeport, died on March 13, 1849, at the age of ninety-six. His only offspring, daughter Ruby Mack, survived him by only eight months. The Trumbull reservation had been wracked by arson and "mismanagement" and the intention of the overseer to sell it off had been made known. It was a time when new leadership was clearly needed, and a new locale would be needed as well for the seat of power.

The South End settlement was approaching its apogee as adjudged by the 1850 Collins & Clark map. The Freeman and Jackson/Deming clans were dominant in the community both numerically and in terms of wealth. Joel Freeman's sisters were becoming active participants in the real estate boom from their residence in New York City, fifty-eight miles distant. Presence Jackson was employed in the household of P.T. Barnum, who was himself an in-law of new tribal overseer Dwight Morris. A sachem politically palatable to both leading families would be needed to hold the Paugussett community in balance.

That individual appears to have been Rensselaer Pease. He was the son-in-law of Ruby Mack and exhibited throughout his life a responsibility that appears to have been lacking in his wife Nancy and some other of her associates. He was also almost certainly the father of William Sherman, direct lineal descendant of Tom Sherman and therefore "heir apparent" to the sachemhood.

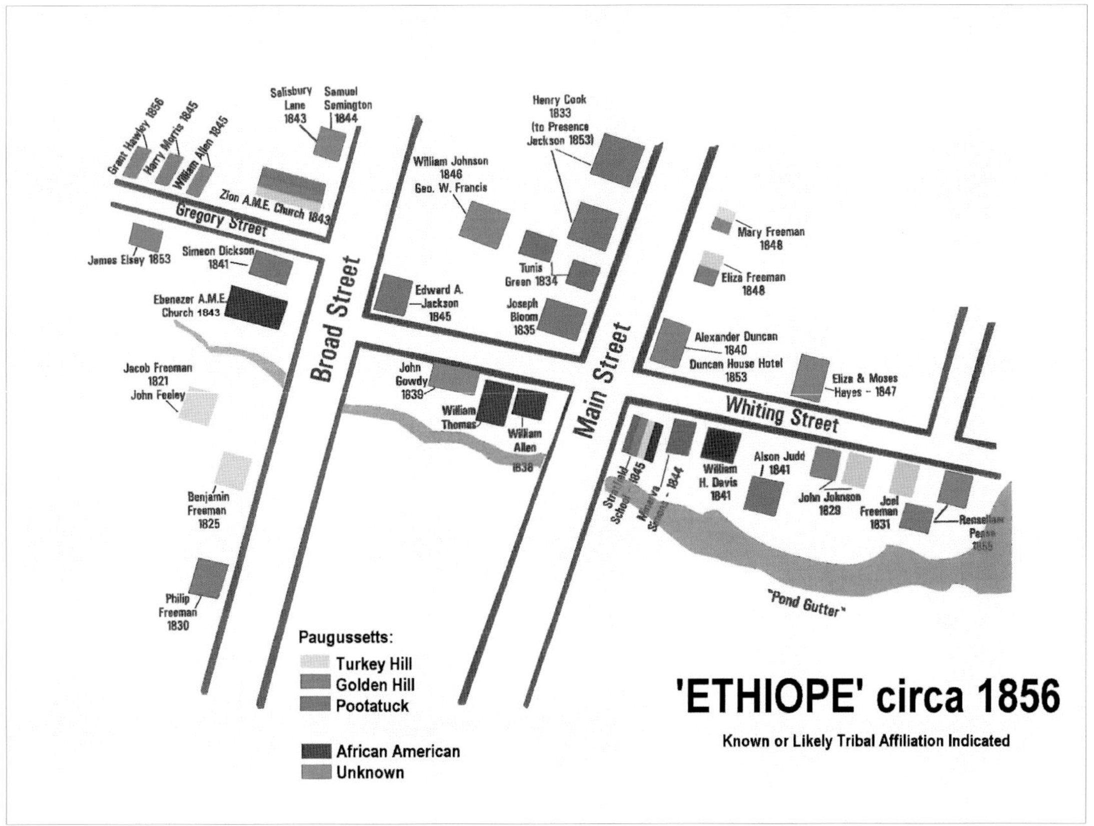

The Ethiope/Liberia Community at its apogee, circa 1855.

In 1850, Rensselaer Pease was about forty-three years of age. He had ties to the Jackson family,[199] and also to the Freemans.[200], as well as other influential members of the community—Simeon Dixon and Philander Pitts were in-laws,[201] and Tunis Green was his uncle. As if to solidify the unity of the tribe, Rensselaer Pease took up residence in Joel Freeman's house shortly after the 1850 census.

In 1853, what was to become the economic engine of the South End community began to take shape—the great Duncan House Hotel. Although it can not be proven in the public record, it is thought that the major impetus behind its development was Joel Freeman's sister Mary, who was at that point chef in a New York City hotel. The hotel's namesake, Alexander Duncan, was a prominent New York businessman and investor. The hotel would employ a substantial segment of the South End's working population and provide a market for farmers and fishermen in the outlying areas.

At about this very same time the Freeman family in North Stratford began to expand its landholdings and venture into the commercial farming business. James Farm was transformed from uninhabited countryside into prosperous homesteads under the leadership of George Freeman. Like his likely kinsman Joel, he was a man of wealth and vision who made loans to fellow community members, served as witness at important functions and provided burial space to known Paugussetts in his cemetery plot in the shadow of his huge monument. He can be seen as a second village sagamore under the suzerainty of the tribal sachem.

And in Derby, the Phillips, Moses and Alling families made up the third group of Paugussett clans. In the 1840s and '50s, they, too, joined the rural exodus, leaving their isolated hilltop and establishing their residence in the factory town at Ansonia in the valley below.

There may have been other clan settlements as well. In Newtown, the Purdy and Edwards families provided loan funds for the Bridgeport community, suggesting some form of economic success that has not as yet been explored. It is known that other tribal members resided at New Milford/Bridgewater, Woodbury and Litchfield during this period.

Rensselaer Pease died on April 24, 1856, a victim of consumption (within a few short years his brother Levi, sister Laura and daughter Olive would meet the same fate). The South End community suffered some severe blows at this time, and in the records that survive there is some suggestion of a struggle for primacy between its two leading clans.

P.T. Barnum's great house, Iranistan, was burned to the ground, and in the aftermath of the financial Panic of 1857 the showman was plunged into bankruptcy. Presence Jackson was thus turned out of her influential position and had to seek out other work. The hotel project became a financial boondoggle, and it seems as though Mary Freeman may have borne some of the blame. For some unknown reason, she chose to leave the church that her brother had founded, and took instruction and was baptized a member of the First Methodist Church (a solidly white congregation) in 1858. Apparently, other members[202] left with her. Joel Freeman died of syphilis in 1865; it is not known how long this debilitating illness may have affected his ability to provide leadership to the Bridgeport community. What is known is that John Deming became head trustee of the church as well as treasurer and superintendent of the Sunday school; his wife Ellen assumed control of the women's group Daughters of Zion.

The Retreat from the City

William Sherman's first "a count" with tribal overseer Dwight Morris is written in his own hand in 1857, the very first line in what was apparently a brand new notebook. This date coincides with the birth record of his son in the town of Trumbull and the date Orcutt maintains he became sexton of the Nichols Farms cemetery. It also appears to indicate that William felt it prudent to remove himself from Bridgeport (where he is recorded as a resident in 1847 and 1853) shortly after assuming the mantle of leadership. William was then thirty-two years old and, as noted earlier, was in a direct line of descent from the historic Paugussett sachems. His choice of location at Nichols Farms may have been due to its location central to the communities at Ansonia (Derby), North Stratford and Bridgeport, or it may be related to the prior site of the 1842–54 reservation. It may also be that he wished to live in proximity to Franklin Ambler, who may have been the mentor who taught him to read and write (Rensselaer Pease did not have this ability).

William's interaction with the tribal membership is recorded in the journal he kept from 1873 to 1879, and sporadically through other periods. We know of his dealings with John Cam, George Freeman, George Purdy and Henry O. Pease, whom he refers to as "Henry Sherman" on occasion. We have learned the identities of "Drake," "John Weston," and others who also appear to be Paugussetts. They constitute evidence that there was very much a community that functioned together during this period.

Sherman is less specific about his relationship with the Bridgeport community. "Went to Bridgeport" is recorded numerous times without explanation. We know he was in attendance at community picnics every year, and we know his son married Jane Phoenix, daughter of the minister of the Bridgeport church.[203] This is in and of itself ample indication of the social standing of the Sherman family and establishes that William was no mean farm and turnpike worker in the eyes of his community.

To secure a land base for the tribe, or at the very least for its leadership, appears to have been a life goal of William Sherman. He worked tirelessly and was at last able to buy a lot barely big enough to construct a house. There was no woodlot attached to provide for winter heating needs, no pasture space for a cow and little provision for even a rudimentary vegetable garden. William and his successors would not be able to maintain self-sufficiency on this miniscule parcel, but at least it would be something that was inviolable. William's granddaughter Ethel, Chieftess Rising Star, would speak more than a hundred years later of how her grandmother had emphasized the importance of the tiny reservation: "Always protect the land. Always come back to the land." It is known that some tribal members were buried on the back part of the reservation, a place where it dips down toward a wetland. This is probably a conscious continuation of the practice that had made the earlier Golden Hill Reservation in Bridgeport a much-hallowed place in tribal annals.

In the pages of the journal, we glimpse William working on the construction of his home. He was a man in his fifties, an elderly person by the standards of his day, and he was reputed to have weighed in the neighborhood of 360 pounds. And yet he persevered, with the help of other Paugussett workers, and completed his dwelling in good order. He was able to enjoy the fruits of his labor for a decade. Shortly before his passing, perhaps when he felt the imminence of his death, he did what was necessary to keep the property out of the hands of squabbling heirs and in the possession of the tribe as a whole, to serve as a symbol and the sole remnant of the vast territory they once had controlled, as well as a reminder of the reservation lands his ancestors had been promised in perpetuity. He used his power as chief of the Paugussett tribe to reestablish the Golden Hill Reservation.

The Urban Indians

To return to the various communities of Paugussett tribal members, the South End of Bridgeport was burgeoning as new industries came to the city and Paugussett people became an integral part of the city's economic life. We have discussed that the Doric

Lodge of the Masonic fraternity was established in 1871 (its leadership was solidly Native American, the majority Paugussett). And we know from accounts of this time that this organization assumed the role of a police force in the community.

The Deming family retained its leadership role in Zion Church. It is known that, together with Presence Jackson, they secured a huge loan ($5,200) against their property as another depression fell upon the country,[204] perhaps utilized to keep their people afloat economically. Ellen Deming's group, the Daughters of Zion, provided money for the reconstruction of Zion Church in 1882, and church tradition relates that the congregation met in the Demings's home while the new building was being constructed. Presence Jackson's one-time employer P.T. Barnum was enticed to be the keynote speaker at the dedication ceremony of the new church and provided a generous contribution to erase a significant portion of the church debt.

Mary Freeman, the last of her clan in the South End following Joel's death in 1865, appears to have been at odds with the majority of her community. The news item that appeared in the *Bridgeport Standard* of July 1, 1882, tells us that she was barely spared a lynching after the fatal fire in one of her rental properties, and a number of residents testified against her at a coroner's inquest. She died in 1883, her huge estate bequeathed at the last moment, under highly suspect circumstances, to the physician that was tending her.

The Bridgeport community became overwhelmed as their village on the far outskirts of town was at first physically incorporated and then made a part of the inner city. The church remained its focal point, although African Americans again came to join its ranks. In the late nineteenth century, there was no Simeon Dickson to plead for the purity of the Indian community and no new partition of the congregation. The Daughters of Zion remained an organization comprised entirely of Native American women through the mid–twentieth century, however, and will be discussed shortly.

The Derby community, which became part of the newly established city of Ansonia in 1889, blossomed anew during this period. Located just under nine miles from the reservation in Trumbull (the South End community in Bridgeport was slightly less than seven miles distant), the community actually expanded and consolidated as the century drew to a close. The Phillips and Alling/Allen families were married into the Tinney line. They collectively left the Episcopal Church in Derby at the time the Clinton A.M.E. Church was established in the 1890s, and have existed as a tightknit enclave until the present day. They, too, will be discussed with the twentieth century.

The Twentieth Century

William Sherman's second-oldest son George succeeded his father as leader of the Paugussett tribe and occupant of the Trumbull reservation. Apparently his older brother William, who had become a skilled mechanic, did not wish to uproot himself from the city and take responsibility for the well-being of the entire tribe. After a brief period of residence in Derby, William was to live out his life in Bridgeport.

A brief note is in order regarding the status of the reservation in the period between 1886 and 1933. William Sherman had left the property to the tribal overseer in trust for the Golden Hill Paugussett tribe. The overseer in 1886 was Rowland B. Lacey of Bridgeport. Following Lacey's death in 1897, startling revelations were an almost daily feature in Bridgeport newspapers of how this "pillar of the community" had pilfered various estates and trust funds left in his care. The records of the Golden Hill Trust Fund disappeared under his stewardship, as did the evidence of his perfidy of various other estates and charities. No restitution was ever offered the tribe. Perhaps embarrassed, or perhaps wishing to forget the entire matter, the State of Connecticut did not appoint a successor, and the tribe was basically left to fend for itself.

We do know that as George Sherman became cognizant of his special rights as a Native American, he made the Town of Trumbull aware that he was not liable for real estate taxes. As noted earlier, he proudly told a *Bridgeport Post* reporter in 1927 about his special privileges, which included hunting and fishing out of season without a permit, and the lack of necessity for licensing his dog.

George did not maintain a good relationship with his daughter Ethel, and as a result we have a wealth of documentation beginning in the 1920s as she demanded that the state live up to its obligations to the tribe. She also demanded, as a bona fide Golden Hill Indian, that she be allowed access to the reservation, something her father had denied her. It is significant that she did not ask for control of the property, but only access. Ethel was widely regarded as a woman who embodied Native American spirituality, and by her own testimony in later years it seems that her grandmother had inculcated in her at a young age the vital importance of this land, sacred as a spiritual focus and a place where Paugussett dead lay buried.

By 1933, the State of Connecticut was beginning to reassert its responsibility for all four of its recognized tribes, and that included the Golden Hill Paugussetts. In that year, Connecticut formalized the status of the reservation, and in impressive ceremonies—which included representatives of Native American tribes from across America—Ethel was installed as Chieftess Rising Star.

With the death of George Sherman, Ethel's brother Edward was also elevated to the chieftainship, and he assumed the name Chief Black Hawk. Like his father, he was well known in the Bridgeport and Valley communities as a spokesman for the American Indian and a keeper of important traditions. In the public eye and in the opinion of many tribal members, however, he appears to have been much overshadowed by his sister the chieftess.

The chieftess was to become a woman of some wealth, and there are many testimonies that she used her financial resources to assist those tribal members in need. She fell into the role of clan mother by taking young girls under her wing and educating them in the traditions of her people. As previously noted, she was a tireless advocate for Indian rights and wrote letters to the governor, the president and, frequently, the editor of the newspaper. In one instance, she bristled upon being called a "self-styled" chieftess in print, and rebutted the remark with a delineation of her credentials. She was known for always appearing in public wearing Indian dress, and it is clear from photographs that survive from this period that many of her fellow tribe members did likewise. She

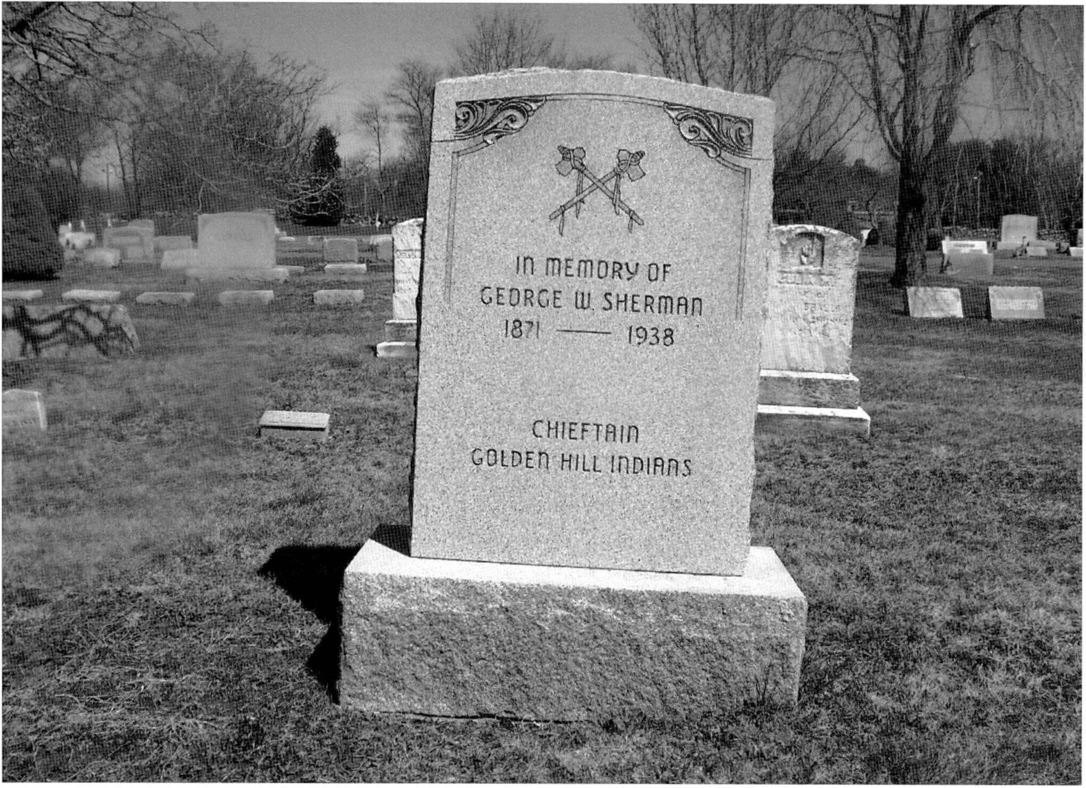

George Sherman's grave marker, Nichols Farms Cemetery.

made friends with leaders of other Indian nations, and we have the record of Sitting Bull's grandson being invited to her twice-weekly council meetings. The chieftess's home during the 1930s was on Harral Avenue in Bridgeport, immediately adjacent to the pre-1802 Golden Hill Reservation. (In the early 1950s she moved to Chopsey Hill Road at Platt Street, immediately adjoining the pre-1802 Rocky Hill Indian lot.)

During this period, the Bridgeport community was apparently becoming submerged by the expanding African American population. As the Paugussetts became a minority in their own church, many left and became affiliated with St. Mark's Episcopal Church, on Newfield Avenue. The pastor of St. Mark's, Reverend Cuffee, was a member of the Shinnecock tribe from Long Island.

Bridgeport's Indians retained community, but more and more they were welcoming members of other tribes to their ranks. One local woman, Maisa Tisdale, researched her family tree and learned from her great-aunt that the great-aunt's mother would meet every Monday with "Indian women," and discuss their common problems and other matters of importance. The name of this group was the Daughters of Zion.

This woman died on July 22, 1943, and the funeral sign-in book that survives provides a window into the Bridgeport Indian community that existed at that time. There are Paugussett family names (Mitchell, Gibson, Richardson, Freeman and Randolph [married into the Tinney line]), Schaghticoke names (Harris, Hodge), Mahican (Berry, Wilson, Van Allen), Nehantic (Beamon, Brooks, Mason), Narragansett (Cozzins) and Mohegan (Hamilton). This shows us that while the Paugussett community survived in this city, as it indeed survives to the present day, its influence became diluted as the city grew and diversified.

Chieftess Rising Star appears to have especially favored the Paugussett community in Ansonia with her attention. The tribe's oral histories testify over and over how she would take the bus to town and spend her weekends paying calls on the membership. She would converse at length with family elders, but seemed to go out of her way to inculcate to the children the importance of tribal identity and the history of the relationship to the land. At the end of her visit she would habitually reach into her bag and produce gifts for each member of the younger generation.

The Ansonia community basically became known as the "Tinney line" shortly after the turn of the twentieth century. A well-remembered leader was Fred Tinney, "Chief One Leaf," who had an affinity for his Indian heritage second only to that of the chieftess. Countless photographs of the man from youth to old age show him in Indian attire. He owned a piece of land in the vicinity of Prospect Street that was the setting for family gatherings and the teaching of Indian lore to the children of the tribal community.

The Tinneys were clustered in the old Fourth Ward of Ansonia, in the vicinity of Main and Factory Streets. Into this neighborhood of working-class multifamily homes moved Aurelius Piper, son of Chieftess Rising Star, during the 1940s, thus solidifying the bonds with the reservation. The Tinneys and the Pipers were interrelated, and together formed a tightknit community united by their Native American heritage.

Chieftess Rising Star elevated Aurelius to the position of chief at a ceremony in 1959. Named "Big Eagle," he was to assume a pivotal role in tribal survival and regeneration in the years that followed. Chief Big Eagle conducted programs in the city schools of Bridgeport to acquaint young students with the beliefs and practices of the Native Americans, and to make them aware of the continuing Indian presence in Connecticut. He later became a spiritual counselor in the state prison system, focusing his outreach on Native American inmates. On October 11, 1984, Big Eagle founded the White Buffalo Society, "a Native American Religious Order and wildlife sanctuary." He continues to function as spiritual leader of that organization.

When Edward Sherman, Chief Black Hawk, died in 1974, Chief Big Eagle assumed the central role in the tribe. The record of activity becomes substantial at this point. Tribal gatherings at the reservation became commonplace. Sweat lodges were conducted openly for the first time, and young people from the communities in Bridgeport and Ansonia were brought to the chief to learn the ways of their people. Weddings, christenings and name-bestowing ceremonies became a frequent occurrence at the reservation under the new chief's impetus to reignite his tribe.

During the 1970s, newsletters came to be published for the entire membership on a regular basis. Council meetings became organized affairs, and minutes were taken. Chief Big Eagle was appointed to the Connecticut Indian Affairs Council in 1974 along with representatives of the state's other recognized tribes. He also served as member of the board of directors and treasurer of American Indians for Development. Virtually every tribal member would spend time on the reservation, a far cry from the situation decried by the chief's mother in the 1920s and '30s.

Great notoriety came to the Golden Hill Paugussetts beginning in the 1970s, as wealthy suburbanite neighbors of the reservation became alarmed at the increasing level of activity and sought "legal" means of seizing the property. Chief Big Eagle stood his ground as the nation watched and emerged victorious after almost superhuman efforts on his part. Big Eagle also sought, and obtained, funds from the U.S. Department of Housing and Urban Development to secure land for the tribe in the town of Colchester, Connecticut, where it was hoped that at last the membership could develop a traditional community.

Well into his seventies, and nearing exhaustion from his trials, Big Eagle became the "traditional" chief of his people in 1990, and the active leadership was passed to his son Aurelius Jr., Chief Quiet Hawk. Quiet Hawk made the granting of recognition by the federal government a priority and has galvanized the membership in this effort. Many volumes of records have documented the activities of Quiet Hawk's administration and demonstrate a level of involvement that has grown with each passing year. Communication is constant, and the tribe is unified as never before in this pursuit.

Thus we see that tribal leadership has continued without a single significant break from the time of the Golden Hill Reservation in Bridgeport (and, prior to that, to the period of first contact) down to the present time. The membership has always comprised a community, cognizant of its common heritage and bonds across the centuries, collectively aware of each individual's responsibility to the common good. This, in short, is continuity.

14.

Tribal Administration—the Twentieth Century

Chief Big Eagle maintains a volume of collected nuggets of information about the Paugussett tribe. One inclusion, from Report 30 of the Bureau of American Ethnology (1911–12),[205] presents the history of the tribe as it was seen in the first years of the twentieth century, as well as its status in that day:

> **Paugusset** *("where the narrows open out"—Trumbull). A small Algonquian tribe in Connecticut, on the Housatonic r., near the mouth of the Naugatuck. Their principal village, Paugusset, was on the e. side of the river. They had a fortress on the e. bank about half a mile above the Naugatuck, and another in Milford. Ruttenber makes them a part of the Wappinger confederacy, and says they were subject to the Mattabesec. They claimed a tract on both sides of the lower Housatonic, extending up to Newtown, but sold most of their lands about 1660. Besides their principal village they had Turkey Hill Village, Pauquaunuch, Naugatuck, and Poodatook. The whole tribe numbered perhaps 700 or 800. In 1762 they had mainly retired to Scaticook, farther up the river, where the survivors then numbered 127, while about 60 were still in their old homes. Several mixed-blood families are said to survive near Bridgeport, Conn.*

These "several mixed-blood families" comprised one of America's earliest tribes to be almost completely urbanized. Rather than living in teepees on the vastness of the open prairie, the Paugussetts lived mainly in cramped apartments in the tenements of Bridgeport and Ansonia, two of Connecticut's major industrial centers. They were employed as cooks, draymen and factory workers, working long hours at difficult jobs in the interest of survival. Like members of Connecticut's other tribes, the vast majority of the Paugussetts lived "off-reservation," yet retained consciousness of their ancient Native American heritage and identity through frequent contact with the tribal leadership, gatherings at weddings, funerals and christenings, and periodic visits with one another.

Also in common with other Connecticut tribes, the reservation remained more of a symbolic link with the past than a place of communal dwelling for a majority of the membership. One census of the state's reservations shows that the Golden Hill Paugussett Reservation consisted of "1 lot" with a population of two; the Eastern Pequot reservation contained 220 acres and eleven inhabitants; the Western Pequots (Mashantucket) held on to 184 acres and just two people; and "Scaticook [sic]" extended to 400 acres with a population of zero.

We know that the tribe remained active from a variety of sources. Books, periodicals and newspaper accounts provide information about tribal leadership and continuity for each decade during the twentieth century. Indian identity became a source of pride rather than embarrassment, and obituaries, marriage announcements and the like often imparted this information about tribal members. For example, the obituary of William Sherman's daughter Mary, which appeared in the *Bridgeport Evening Post* of November 28, 1905, refers to her as "a full blooded Indian and a descendant of the Golden Hill Tribe." We also have the photographic records of a number of prominent Paugussett families, which reveal that they embraced their Native American identity and made it a focus of their lives. We have the recollections of tribal elders (preserved through the tribe's oral histories), which verify and amplify what the photographic and printed record tells us about the continued survival of the Paugussett people. And, finally, we have the official records of the interactions between the State of Connecticut and the Tribal leadership, many of whom were at least for a time residents on the "1 lot."

As delineated in another portion of this treatise, the final overseer of the Golden Hill Paugussett tribe was Rowland B. Lacey, who served until his death on March 31, 1897. Described as "one of the best known and most highly respected citizens of Bridgeport" in his *Bridgeport Evening Post* obituary, Lacey posthumously achieved a degree of infamy following revelations that surfaced regarding fiscal mismanagement in accounts for which he served as trustee (or, in the tribe's case, overseer). With no Golden Hill Tribal Fund left to administer, and no indigent tribe members needing to be cared for, the State of Connecticut allowed matters to drift until they were called severely to account by Chieftess Rising Star in the late 1920s and early 1930s.

We do know that Connecticut maintained a government-to-government relationship with the tribe during this period despite its failure to appoint new overseers. The state legislature annually reaffirmed the June 19, 1876 "Act concerning the Support of the Golden Hill Tribe of Indians":

> **Golden Hill tribe of Indians.** *In any case where the income received by the overseer of the Golden Hill tribe of Indians for the lands or money belonging to that tribe, shall be insufficient for their support, so that any member of said tribe is, or is likely to be, chargeable as a pauper in any town, the superior court for the county of Fairfield may, upon the application of the selectmen of such town, after due notice to said overseer, and after hearing the parties, order said overseer to sell such proportion of the property of said tribe as the number of members so chargeable may bear to the whole number of said tribe, and to pay over the proceeds of such sale, together with a like proportion of any other money*

> *in his control belonging to such tribe, to the selectmen of such town, with authority to said town to use the whole or any part thereof for the support of such member or members of said tribe so chargeable as shall be named in such order* [wording of statute between 1902 and 1918].

Newspaper accounts give us some insight into life on the reservation in the first decades of the last century. The *Bridgeport Sunday Post* of February 27, 1927, featured an article on the history of the Golden Hill tribe and the inhabitants of the reservation in that year: "[William's] son George, who married Nancy A. Hamilton, is living on the ancestral farm at Nichols, and although he is ultramodern in his views and outlook on life, retains something of the quiet dignity and pose of the illustrious men who once peopled the land whereon Bridgeport now stands."

The *Bridgeport Sunday Post* of August 23, 1931, tells us:

> *Hunting and fishing with immunity at any time of the year in defiance of the laws of the State of Connecticut are the proud privileges of George W. Sherman of Nichols. Also, he is never called upon to pay taxes, nor is it necessary for him to get a license for his dog, when he has one. The reasons are simple, for he is a Pequonnock Indian. And, as such, he has certain freedoms that do not hold for the white man.*

This article goes on to tell of George's fruit and vegetable stand that provided his means of livelihood. It also pictures him "wearing his Indian costume," and provides evidence of the survival of Paugussett traditions. When his beloved dog died, "He gave him the same last rites that would be given any well-born Indian warrior." There is also some information regarding the burial ground known to exist on the tiny reservation:

> *Sherman informed the writer that there was a small Indian cemetery about 100 feet from his present home on which he still calls the Golden Hill reservation. He said that he was able to find at least five graves with markers indicating that they were extremely old. Some time ago, he said, he discovered that vandals had raided the cemetery and ransacked two graves. It was his opinion that it was done by college students who had learned of the place. Sherman said that he could recall when his father took him to visit the cemetery when he was but a wee tot. He said it was as a result of these visits that he was able to find any traces of the place today.*

George Sherman's understanding of his special rights is illustrated by former Trumbull Town Attorney Aaron Levine's reminiscence that appeared in the *Trumbull Times* on December 1, 1976:

> [Levine] *grew up on Shelton Road, just across the way from the quarter-acre tract that is being disputed now. Among his memories, Mr. Levine recalled the time around 1916 when George Sherman…and his father, the late Samuel Levine, went fishing in the Trap Falls Reservoir in Shelton. Unfortunately, it wasn't legal, but Mr. Sherman*

convinced Mr. Levine that he knew a spot where not only were the fish biting, but where they couldn't possibly be seen by the game warden. He was right about the first aspect, but wasn't quite accurate about the second. The game warden not only caught them, but he arrested them, too.

Came the day of the trial and Mr. Levine arrived ready to pay the fine, went the narrative, but not Mr. Sherman. Instead he arrived at the courthouse in full Indian regalia, feathers and paint and all. The judge looked quizzically at Mr. Sherman and asked what it was about before he imposed sentence. Mr. Sherman said that, as a Native American, living on a federal reservation, he was not subject to state law. The judge, recalled the younger Mr. Levine who was then about eight years old, was reluctant to challenge Mr. Sherman's contention and, not wishing to create an incident with an Indian, threw his case out of court. But Mr. Levine had to pay his fine.

George Sherman died December 28, 1938, at the age of seventy-seven. The *Bridgeport Telegram* gave him a prominent obituary replete with a photograph—once again in full Indian regalia.

During the late 1920s and early 1930s George's daughter Ethel began to press demands that the reservation be opened to her and other members of the tribe. A 1933 newspaper story says of their tumultuous relationship, "For years there have been disagreements between them." Ethel retained the services of an attorney, and at her insistence the State of Connecticut finally appointed a successor to Rowland B. Lacey, who had died thirty-six years previous:

Raymond Beckwith, constable, of Trumbull, has been appointed "overseer" of the Golden Hill Indians at their reservation in Trumbull by Judge John Richards Booth in Superior Court, on the application of Ethel Sherman Piper Baldwin, the daughter of George Sherman, the aged head of the tribe. The application was made through Attorney Earl Smith. Overseer Beckwith is under a $1,000 bond, furnished today. The application and the appointment point to the final chapter of a vanishing tribe of Indians that held full sway over the territory in which Bridgeport is located... [Bridgeport Telegram, July 18, 1933].

The *Bridgeport Post* of that same date accounted for the period following Lacey's death in 1897: "Since that time, the remnants of the tribe have managed their own affairs."

On October 3, 1933, the reservation was the scene of the triumphant installation of Ethel as "Chieftess Rising Star." The *Post* described the event, and sent a photographer to record the festivities:

With the Chieftess on her visit were the Princesses, White Wing and Red Wing, sisters and members of the Winnebago Indians from Nebraska and Chief Reindeer of the Shoshone Indians from Wyoming. The group reached Nichols in a large touring car, dressed in Indian regalia. They carried robes, tom toms, peace pipes, and other necessary requisites for the ceremony. Passing motorists as well as residents viewed the function with great wonderment, and of course were made to realize that Sherman truly was of Indian blood. Arriving at the reservation, the group viewed the grounds, posed for photographs, and the tribunal medicine song was played by Princess White Wing on her tom toms. She also sang Indian rituals. Princess White Wing and Red Wing, as well as Chief Reindeer, came to Bridgeport from New York and stopped at the home of Rising Star [425 Harral Avenue]. *They had attended an Indian Day meeting [emphasis added] where Princess Rising Star was recognized as Chieftess of the Golden Hill Reservation in Nichols.*

The *Bridgeport Post* of May 11, 1939, referred to Ethel as a "self-styled" Chieftess. On May 17 of that year they printed her response:

To the Editor:

I read in your paper recently the description of "self-styled Chieftess of the reservation at Nichols" in relation to myself. I have spent much time in thought. You say that I, Ethel Lillanonah Baldwin am a self-styled Chieftess Rising Star of the Golden Hill reservation at Nichols, Connecticut. I write to tell you you are wrong. I received my name at a big feast. My name was called many times. It was my father's desire and his wish after receiving my papers that I be made Chieftess of the Golden Hill reservation. He was there to see me reopen our Indian land as the Chieftess in October 1933. The life of a chief among the Indians is much different than the life of a chief in your white race. Circumstances and individual natures and abilities determine the power and sway of Indian chiefs and chieftesses. The Indian chiefs are not full of greed. We do not go about to make trouble for others. I am not interested in the dispute over the reservation in Trumbull. The dangers and all the troubles I passed through have been forgotten. I have my papers for the Indian lands. I do not care to live there, but I can go there any time I wish. I go there, I love my own beautiful land. An Indian chief is not land hungry.

The role of overseer passed to the State Park and Forestry Commission in 1935. On February 17, 1939, the *Post* reported that the Nichols Village Improvement Association was petitioning the state to "get rid of" the Indian reservation (its long-time occupant, George Sherman, had recently died). "Members claim that the site, with an old building located in the middle of it, is no asset to the village," according to the piece. On May 25 of that year, the Connecticut Attorney General Francis A. Pallotti issued a report to the State Park and Forest Commission. He found that "the title [to the property] appears still to vest *in the tribe.*" He went on to opine:

When an individual Indian has obtained title to land without restrictions or conditions as to alienation, he may sell it as any other person.

An individual Indian may, therefore, sell and convey real estate in this state as any other person, excepting land "belonging to, or which has belonged to, the estate of any tribe."

William Sherman acquired title in fee simple to the land in question from Charles Ambler, and by the quit claim deed from William Sherman to Ro[w]*land B. Lacey, Agent of the Golden Hill Tribe, title to said land vested in the Agent as Trustee of the Golden Hill Tribe. It does not appear that it was conveyed to be held in trust for the benefit of William Sherman or his son George M. Sherman individually.*

...Section 1587c of the 1935 Cumulative Supplement authorizes the State Park and Forest Commission to act as overseer of all tribes of Indians residing in this State and empowers said Commission to "sell or exchange any real or personal property belonging to any member of any such tribe of Indians."

You will observe that the latter provision authorizes the Commission to sell lands belonging to any member of such tribe. It does not authorize the Commission to sell land belonging to Indian tribes. The land in question does not belong to "any member" of the Golden Hill Tribe, but is held as tribal land in the name of the Agent, as Trustee for the Golden Hill Tribe of Indians. We are of the opinion that the State Park and Forest Commission does not have authority to sell the land in question.

The land was not in fact sold, to the vexation of the Nichols Village Improvement Association. It came to be occupied by the Chieftess's brother, Edward L. Sherman, Chief Black Hawk. Also at this time, a photograph of Aurelius Piper Sr. appeared in the *Bridgeport Post*, standing alongside his mother, the chieftess, in a naval uniform. Headlined "Indian in Navy," it was captioned in part "Aurelius Henry Piper, a full blooded Algonquin Indian, has recently completed his basic training at the Naval Training station, Newport, R.I."

In 1941, responsibility for Connecticut's reservation Indians was shifted to the Commissioner of Welfare. Annual reports on the conditions at the Golden Hill Reservation provide information about the activities of the occupants and repair work required on the building, but give little detail about how the tribe functioned as a whole.

For this period, then, we must rely on the oral histories provided by tribal members to see the full measure of activity that involved the Paugussett community. Chief Quiet Hawk (born 1945) recounts how he would meet his grandmother, Chieftess Rising Star, when she got off the bus at Main and Factory Streets in Ansonia:

From there my grandmother and I would walk to the homes of our tribal members—the Tinneys, Williamses, and others. I was very young, but I could tell the conversations were serious. Rising Star spoke with them about what she was doing on the reservation, how important it was for them to respect the land, the traditions, culture, and heritage of the tribe. She was always concerned with how they were getting along and often spoke of the sadness she had in her heart that they couldn't all live together on the Tribe's reservation because it was only ¼ acre, therefore impossible at the time for everybody to live together on. There wasn't even enough room to have tribal members join together on the reservation to have meetings—particularly since during those days they could not meet outside, but rather had to gather and hold ceremonies "behind closed doors," so as not to be ostracized by outsiders. That is why our visits to tribal members were so important.

My grandmother carried two large shopping bags along with her pocket book. She was always dressed in Indian-style clothing [which was her normal dress]*; she never or very rarely wore "white women's clothing," especially when carrying out tribal business. In the shopping bags Rising Star carried money and other items that she distributed among the tribal members.*

...There was nothing more important to her than teaching tribal members—whether they be child or adult—about the ways of our people. She instilled in everyone to never forget who they were and that it was up to every member to teach and carry on the traditions of the Tribe from one generation to the next.

On her one-hundredth birthday, Ethel was to recall, "I've worked hard all my life. If I saw someone who was sick or needed help, I was there for them."[206] Her son was equally involved in the welfare of the tribe. California tribal member Grant Felldin recalls that Chief Black Hawk made a trip to the west coast "to meet with tribal members here." (Florence Mattier collaborates this information and remembers that it took place in 1957.)

In the Ansonia community there are testimonies of Paugussett tribesmen born as early as 1912 recounting their consciousness of Native American identity and community. One woman, Gail Stanley, explains some of the inner workings of this group that were closed to newspaper reporters and state welfare officials:

When I was a little girl my pa [Harold Tinney] *used to take my sisters and I for rides every Sunday and tell us about the lands that were taken from the Indians in the Valley—up the river and in the Naugatuck area.*

I remember going to some type of powwow in Ansonia on Prospect Street. I remember wearing some type of Indian dress with feathers; I remember the teepee and the smoke and seeing other Indians. I believe the land at that time belonged to my uncle, Frederick Tinney. He went to a lot of Indian affairs and would share stories with our family. My Uncle Fred, as we called him, always encouraged us to be proud of our Indian heritage.

...I also remember when my Uncle Fred and his brother, my Uncle Norman [Nonney], *died, tribal members came, and there was some type of ceremony done at both funerals.*

Albums of photographs maintained by the Tinney family from the turn of the twentieth century bear witness to their strong Native American identify and to the persistence of Paugussett tribal traditions.

An article in the *Bridgeport Sunday Herald* of February 25, 1951, described the tragic suicide/homicide of Julia Baldwin Farrar, daughter of Chieftess Rising Star, and her newborn child. She was described as "an authentic Indian princess;" her mother as "an outspoken champion of Indian rights."

The *Bridgeport Telegram* of April 26, 1968, ran a story on Edward Sherman (pictured again in Indian dress), then a month short of his eightieth birthday. It stated in part:

Although Mr. Sherman, who holds the honorary title "Chief Black Hawk," was always conscious of his heritage, he never felt it made him a second-class citizen, a problem which plagues many Indians on the larger western reservations. Only once did it have an effect on his life. "That was in 1926, the year we got the right to vote. Then me and my father and Uncle Bill could hit all the saloons. But I remember when I visited the Seminole reservation in the Everglades back in the '30s. Down there I was just 'Indian.' It was the first time I'd ever run into that sort of thing."

...His status as an Indian affords Mr. Sherman some unique privileges. He lives on the reservation rent-free, pays no state taxes, need not apply for a hunting or fishing license and can have any medical expenses or home repairs paid for by the state.

...The story of the state's first inhabitants is drawing to a close, a story in which Edward Sherman of Trumbull is one of the final paragraphs.

Chief Black Hawk died at the age of eighty-five. His obituary[207] called him "leader of the Paugussett Indian nation." The *Hartford Courant*[208] stated, "The Golden Hill tribe has dwindled to fewer than 50 members having the state-required one-eighth Indian blood. Although Mr. Sherman, a half-blood Indian, was called Chief Black Hawk, the tribe's principal spokesman is his nephew, Aurelius Piper of Maine. He has applied to live in the Golden Hill Reservation, a state spokesman said." The *Trumbull Times*[209] noted that Edward was buried "following Indian tradition." At the graveside service, "the coffin was covered with a small colorful blanket on which rested Chief Black Hawk's head-dress." The eulogy was delivered by Chief One Leaf (Fred Tinney of Ansonia), who concluded by proclaiming "that a new chief would replace Chief Black Hawk as...chief of the Golden Hill Indians." That man was Aurelius Piper Sr., Chief Big Eagle.

Chief Big Eagle wrote to Brendan Kelleher, Commissioner of Indian Affairs, on May 21, 1974:

I Aurelius H. Piper, Chief of the Golden Hill Tribe, as of June first will be the official representative of the Golden Hill people. As you know, I have the power of attorney vested to me by the Council and members of the Tribe. I am at any time able to present to the Council or any member of it my power of attorney, and proof if my blood lineage to be the Chief by blood right as those before me. Also, I am able to present at any time the tribal rolls of the Golden Hill people, and my genealogical records as recorded by the State of Connecticut. The blood line for Chief goes back to Ansantaway, and Chief Cockatapane...Tom Sherman was the last original owner of the old Golden Hill Reservation in Bridgeport, Conn. My mother, Mrs. Ethel Sherman, still lives today.

Within a few short months Big Eagle lifted the veil that had kept tribal affairs for the most part in secrecy. "Golden Hill Indians Powwow in Trumbull After 150 Years," headlined a *Bridgeport Post* article on August 13, 1974. It read in part:

Early last month the Golden Hill Tribe of Paugussett Indians met in a tribal meeting on its reservation in Nichols for the first time in more than 150 years. It was done with little notice but with simplicity and following the Indian tradition.

> *...The tribal meeting was evidence that the Golden Hill Indians, led by Chief Big Eagle* [Aurelius H. Piper] *and armed with a state council of Indian Affairs, is becoming increasingly more active and cohesive. The tribe has nearly 100 members. A full 30 adults turned out for the meeting in early July.*

In 1973, Connecticut established the Indian Affairs Council. Early in 1974, an initial oversight was corrected by the state legislature, and a seat on this body was given to the Golden Hill Paugussett tribe (Chief Big Eagle was named his tribe's representative). The legislation behind this act established Connecticut Indians as full citizens for the first time.[210] It also placed the state's tribes under the stewardship of the Department of Environmental Protection, replacing the State Welfare Commission.

The year of 1974 also saw the formation of the American Indian Development Corporation, comprised of Connecticut Indians, which named Chief Big Eagle vice-chairman. This program was intended to find employment and conduct training programs for the state's Native Americans.

In 1976, the Connecticut Department of Finance and Control recommended that the 101-year-old house on the reservation be demolished, and that the chief and his family be moved to state-surplus property at another location. This proved to be the opening volley of a brouhaha that was to pit the chief against town and state officials, and against well-to-do suburbanite neighbors who would have preferred to be rid of the reservation and its tribal gatherings altogether.

The State Department of Environmental Protection agreed to replace the aging structure on the reservation with a new log cabin. After demolition, but before new construction could get underway, a neighbor claimed the property actually belonged to him, and the project was put in limbo. "This Indian is not budging," Big Eagle told the *Bridgeport Post.*[211] On October 27, 1976, the same newspaper reported, "Approximately 100 Connecticut Indians will gather tomorrow at 9 a.m. at the Golden Hill Paugussett Indian Reservation for a spiritual meeting to demonstrate unity with the Golden Hill Indians' impending reservation ownership battle. Activist lawyer William Kunstler is scheduled to address the Indians and will offer his services to the tribe's chief Aurelius (Big Eagle) Piper, central figure in the reservation battle." Big Eagle, despite heart ailments, spent much of the following winter living in a teepee on the reservation with his son, Moon Face Bear, fulfilling his vow to "stay put." November 3, 1976, was a "sharing feast," where members of the tribe and the general public from across the state came together to provide moral and literal support to the chief.

Eventually the state attorney general found the neighbor's land claim invalid and construction resumed on the log structure. The *Trumbull Times* of November 10, 1976, reported, "Prayers to the Earth Mother, the throbs of the drums and the Indian chants were heard all the way to Hartford this past week. And word came back from Governor Grasso's office that Chief Big Eagle would get his log cabin. But not everyone is happy for him, especially several of his neighbors." On November 14, the *Bridgeport Post* quoted one of those neighbors as saying, "This is a nice neighborhood except for the problem with the Indians." Russell Means and Clyde Bellecourt of the American

Indian movement traveled to the reservation to support the chief in his continuing problems with his white neighbors.

A "housewarming" was held for the chief on June 25, 1977, and more than two hundred tribal members, town and state officials and curiosity seekers showed up to celebrate. "Neighbors in the immediate vicinity of the Reservation, members of the group which calls itself the Shelton Road Neighbors, were conspicuously absent," wrote the *Trumbull Times*.

In November 1978, the Golden Hill Paugussett tribe was awarded a grant of $69,000 from the U.S. Department of Housing and Urban Development, followed by a further $45,000 grant in 1980. The funds were used to purchase 108 acres in the town of Colchester, seventy miles to the east of Trumbull, for a "permanent home and cultural center."

This tract was granted formal reservation status by the state legislature in 1981.

In April 1982, Big Eagle officially filed a petition with the U.S. Department of the Interior seeking federal recognition for the Golden Hill Paugussett tribe. He sent a letter requesting assistance to President Ronald Reagan on June 3 of that year. In 1985, the chief told his story of trials and tribulations to Claude Clayton Smith, professor at Virginia Polytechnic Institute. The result was the book *Quarter-Acre of Heartache*. A Dutch anthropologist came to spend two weeks living on the reservation every summer, learning about the chief and the tribe. On August 30, 1987, the *Record-Journal* of Meriden ran a story on the chief, which described his ongoing struggles:

> *As keeper of the Paugussett flame, Piper says he lives as traditional a life as possible. On the reservation he holds dances and sweats, a purification ritual similar to a sauna in which the Indians sit around a fire inside a sweatlodge... "When we have sweats or bonfires everyone gets upset. They don't even like to see me barbecue outside. They listen to these boom boxes all day, yet a quarter-mile down the road our drum bothers them," he said. "I like the woods in the north country. There we can have ceremonies without people calling the law."*

The chief became a spiritual counselor to Native American inmates in Connecticut State Prisons and ran an educational program focusing on Indian heritage in Bridgeport city schools. He became a correspondent covering Eastern tribes for *De Kiva*, a Dutch publication. In addition to the president of the United States, the chief corresponded regularly with Senator Abraham Ribicoff, Governors Ella Grasso and Lowell Weicker and Congressmen Ronald Sarasin and William Ratchford, all on behalf of his tribe.

In 1991, Chief Big Eagle retired to his beloved north country, and issued a proclamation: "I, Aurelius H. Piper, Chief Big Eagle, Chief of the Golden Hill Tribe and the Paugussett Nation, son of Ethel Sherman Piper Baldwin Peters, picked as chief by her in 1959, do hereby say now and for all time that Aurelius H. Piper, Jr., eldest son of Chief Big Eagle, is approved by my hand as Council Chief of the Golden Hill Tribe and Paugussett Indian Nation." Big Eagle thereafter became "Traditional Chief," and semi-retired counsel to the new "Chief of Chiefs."

Aurelius Jr. became Chief Quiet Hawk effective May 1, 1991. His background suited him to the challenges of leading an impoverished urban tribe with its inherent problems. He is an ex-Marine, with a bachelor of arts degree in social welfare and advanced degrees in the same field from Southern Connecticut State University and Boston University. This background would provide him with much of his administration philosophy in dealing with the situation of many of his tribal members.

Myriad examples of the litany of social ills that beset the inner city tribe can be found in the correspondence through the 1990s. The chief was called upon to intervene in cases of child and spousal abuse and drug addiction. He received requests for food and clothing from those eking out an existence at the extreme margins of economic life. There were pleas for help with medical expenses and assistance requests from tribal members who were incarcerated. The chief's actions were in concert with the actions of those who had preceded him—as his grandmother had said, "If I saw someone who was sick or needed help, I was there for them."

Those tribesmen residing on the reservations had it little better. The Sunday *Connecticut Post*[212] ran a story headlined "Conditions on Reservation Bleak for Impoverished Paugussett Indians." It stated, "Recent visits to the reservations in Trumbull and Colchester found some tribe members living in poverty-level conditions, some without electricity or running water." The article went on to describe the circumstances of the twelve residents of the Colchester reservation, with "three long white aluminum-sided trailers and some smaller structures. Only one trailer has running water and electricity. The other residents haul water from a central well head."

At the time he took over the tribe, Chief Quiet Hawk was serving as executive director of American Indians for Development, Inc., the organization his father had helped to form in 1974. On April 23, 1991, he launched the Golden Hill Indian Development Corporation II, with the stated purpose of development of the reservations at Colchester and Trumbull economically and socially, and the pursuance of land claims' issues.

A lawsuit to regain lands taken from the tribe in violation of the federal Nonintercourse Act was launched in September of 1992. The tribe at first sought to reclaim the 12-acre Nimrod Lot and the 8-acre Rocky Hill Lot in the city of Bridgeport, both sold off by the State of Connecticut in 1802 without the stipulated approval of both houses of Congress. In November 1992, they advanced their claim to include the 19¾ -acre Turkey Meadows Reservation in the Town of Trumbull. Concurrently, the tribe sued for repossession of the remainder of the 80-acre Golden Hill Reservation in Bridgeport. Within a fortnight, historic reservation lands in the towns of Milford, Orange, Woodbridge, Stratford and Shelton were added; intent was made known to press claims in twenty-four state municipalities, comprising $44 billion worth of property and 640,000 defendants. News of the lawsuit made front-page news from the *International Herald Tribune* to the *Connecticut Law Review*; Chief Quiet Hawk was quoted as saying "It's a big day in the history of our tribe. I'm exuberant but somewhat melancholy, in that the ancestors can't see this."

Meanwhile, the tribe began to experience a division between Chief Quiet Hawk and his half brother, War Chief Moon Face Bear, of the Colchester reservation. As early as

July 17, 1984, Chieftess Rising Star had felt compelled to write to Connecticut Indian Affairs Coordinator Ed Sarabia:

> *I am Mrs. Ethel Sherman Piper Baldwin Peters, the Clan Mother of the Bear Clan, Golden Hill Indian Tribe, Paugussett Nation. The last full blooded Golden Hill Tribal member born April 2, 1892. I would like to make a statement at this time that Moonface Bear a/k/a Kenneth Piper is not the Chief of the Golden Hill Tribe* [and] *has no right to speak for the members of the Tribe or sign any agreements or treatys* [sic] *for the Golden Hill Tribe. The Chief of the Golden Hill Tribe has been and still is Chief Big Eagle a/k/a Aurelius Piper, appointed by me in the year 1959—Moonface Bear was made Chief in charge of the Colchester Reservation, under Chief Big Eagle. The Chief of the Golden Hill Tribe lives on the Trumbull Reservation, located on Shelton Road, State of Conn., and the only one with my authority to sign or to speak for the Golden Hill Tribe on any matter pertaining to the welfare and the benefit of said Tribe, as we have always had a chieftainship rule.*

In 1993 Moonface Bear began selling tax-free cigarettes from a roadside stand on the Colchester reservation, triggering an armed confrontation with state police. On April 29 of that year, Chief Quiet Hawk and Chief Big Eagle issued a joint statement to tribal members which declared Moonface Bear a renegade and banished him from the Golden Hill Paugussett tribe. Sadly, Chieftess Rising Star had died only five days before this issued statement, after celebrating her centenarian birthday surrounded by her family and tribe members.

Chief Quiet Hawk refocused his attention on bringing the Paugussett tribe into the twenty-first century. He has made continual interaction with all the membership of his far-flung tribe one priority of his administration. Technological advances have made this possible, in contrast with the "once in a lifetime" trip by Edward Sherman to visit Paugussetts on the West Coast. The tribe now communicates regularly and instantly as watts lines and the internet have been incorporated into this strategy. A growing library of videos has kept the membership abreast of ongoing activities, and newsletters have been produced with regularity. Drum ceremonies, educational outings, sweat lodges and the like maintain the spiritual focus at the Trumbull reservation. Powwows conducted by the tribe require more extensive facilities and have usually been held at state parks.

An overriding priority of Chief Quiet Hawk's administration has been the quest for federal recognition. A grant for this purpose was awarded by the secretary of Housing and Urban Development in 1992, and, since that time, many volumes of research have been compiled to form an invaluable body of knowledge on the survival of a small New England tribe. It is to be hoped that, despite innumerable setbacks, this one overriding goal will one day come to fruition.

15.

Conclusion

Finding Joel Freeman's name on a deed that identified him beyond question as a Turkey Hill Paugussett Indian was the slender thread of information that led to a wealth of knowledge about what had been the "missing years" of the nineteenth century. And plotting the places of origin of Ethiope community members on a township map of Connecticut revealed an almost perfect funnel shape, with the wide top between New Milford and Litchfield, tapering neatly down to that section of the coast from Fairfield to Milford—precisely what is generally regarded as the historic territory of the Paugussett tribe.

There is unfortunately no compendium of information of what became of the Indians of Connecticut. We have the tribal leaders' Paugussett-language names on seventeenth- and early eighteenth-century deeds, but later generations appear with common English surnames, with virtually no information of who descended from whom. This is made all the more complicated for the researcher by the apparent need for tribal members' anonymity in the aftermath of the Indian Removal Act as well as the paucity of period information regarding the Ethiope/ Liberia community.

Nevertheless, by painstakingly examining census records, vital records (births, deaths and marriages), land records and lending patterns, probate records and the scant newspaper coverage that was accorded this community during the years in which it flourished, definite patterns emerge. In becoming conversant with the names, familial relationships and occupations of the community membership, a document heretofore thought "worthless" in demonstrating tribal continuity like William Sherman's journal (basically mainly a work log) becomes rife with important information that confirms patterns of interaction.

Rensselaer Pease sharing a house with Joel Freeman, William Sherman's son marrying the daughter of the Zion Church pastor, known Paugussetts dying in a tuberculosis epidemic on the farm of Franklin Ambler's brother-in-law—this putting of two and two together speaks volumes that illustrate time and again that the Paugussett tribe led an active and vibrant existence throughout the nineteenth century, a worthy precursor of the well-documented activity of the twentieth. The leadership of Joel Freeman is indeed demonstrable in the public record, as is his involvement in setting up a church body, reforming it in a "purified" form, petitioning for state school funds, beginning a free lending library and creating a Masonic fraternity and a women's organization. This documentation shows us that there was an active political structure that functioned under his leadership. The Paugussett tribe, in short, did exactly what the federal government requires as proof of tribal continuance and activity can be demonstrated during every decade from 1790 to the present.

For federal acknowledgment, 25 C.F.R. Part 83.7 requires that petitioners must satisfy the following seven criteria:

> *a. The petitioner has been identified as an American Indian entity on a substantially continuous basis since 1900. §83.7(a).*
> *b. A predominant portion of the petitioning group comprises a distinct community and has existed as a community from historical times until the present. §83.7(b).*
> *c. The petitioner has maintained political influence or authority over its members as an autonomous entity from historical times until the present. §83.7(c).*
> *d. It submits to the BAR a copy of the group's present governing document including its membership criteria. §83.7(d).*
> *e. The petitioner's membership consists of individuals who descend from a historical Indian tribe or from historical Indian tribes which combined and functioned as a single autonomous political entity. § 83.7(e).*
> *(The petitioner must provide an official membership list certified by the group's governing body. It must also submit a copy of each available former list of members based on the group's own criterion).*
> *f. The membership of the petitioning group is composed principally of persons who are not members of any acknowledged North American Indian tribe. §83.7(f).*
> *(It can meet the criteria if: (1) the petitioner can establish that it has functioned throughout history until the present as a separately autonomous tribal entity; (2) that its members do not maintain a bilateral political relationship with the acknowledged tribe; and (3) that its members have provided written confirmation of their membership in the petitioning group).*
> *g. Neither the petitioner nor its members are the subject of congressional legislation that has expressly terminated or forbidden the federal relationship. §83.7(g).*

The tribe that saw the futility of a continued woodland existence early on in one of the most industrialized corners of the world, and who went into a growing city and invested in real estate and businesses, fits few people's stereotypes of Native American existence. Nevertheless, this remarkable story is undeniable, and it can readily be confirmed through public documents compiled by the requisite "disinterested third-party sources."

In January 2004, the Golden Hill Paugussett tribe confidently submitted all the information contained in this book to the Bureau of Indian Affairs as definitive proof of its legitimacy. The very day of that transmission—when he could not possibly have known or studied its content—the state attorney general assured the people of Connecticut, "As to the alleged new information…either it isn't new, or it isn't true." And on June 14, 2004, the Bureau of Indian Affairs denied recognition on four of the seven criteria.

The Paugussetts indeed met every one of those seven criteria, demonstrated here chapter and verse. Understandably, after being swindled out of everything from their reservation lands to Mary Freeman's assets to their own tribal fund, they have little reason to have faith in anyone but themselves.

Appendix A

Chronology of Deeds—Early Period (South End Community)

Stratford Land Records

Volume 33, page 341—Sheldon Smith to Seth B. Jones—dwelling house and lot on road running from Episcopal Church to Wells Tongue, $356, May 15, 1820.

Volume 33, page 428—Seth B. Jones to John and Zilpha Feeley of Stratford—undivided half-interest in land and dwelling house and other buildings in Bridgeport bounded east on highway running from the church to Wells Tongue, south and west on property of Timothy Risley, north on heirs of Aaron Hawley, deceased, being a half acre, April 10, 1821.

Volume 33, page 431—Seth B. Jones to Jacob Freeman of Stratford—undivided half-interest in above property, April 10, 1821.

[NOTE: This property had previously been owned by John M. Bouton and conveyed to Sheldon Smith on May 2, 1820 (Stratford Land Records, Volume 33, page 329).]

Bridgeport Land Records

Volume 1, page 237—Timothy Risley to Benjamin Freeman of Bridgeport—thirty-two-rod lot bounded north by Jacob Freeman, east by highway, south and west by grantor, $96, January 13, 1825 (NOTE: Benjamin's wife Dinah died 1843).

Volume 1, page 239—Timothy Risley to Jacob Freeman—eight rods of land "bounded north by said Jacob's home lot," January 13, 1825.

Volume 2, page 280—Seth B. Jones to Isaac Mason—lot at northeast corner Main & Whiting Streets (future site of Duncan House Hotel), $90, February 11, 1828.

Volume 3, page 418—David Curtis to John Johnson—$29\,{}^{4}/_{10}$ rods of land bounded north on Whiting Street, east on Isaac Mason, south on David Curtis land, west "running to a point," $88, November 29, 1829.

Volume 3, page 433—Timothy Risley to Philip Freeman of Fairfield—fifteen rods of land bounded north by Benjamin Freeman, west and south by grantor, east by highway, January 11, 1830.

Volume 4, page 9—Samuel Simons mortgage to Jacob Freeman—a half acre "with buildings thereon standing," April 5, 1832.

Volume 4, page 172—Timothy Risley to Tracey Freeman—$8\,{}^{1}/_{10}$ rods land bounded north by Jacob Freeman and John Felia, west and south by grantor, east by "new street," $20.25, July 1, 1833.

Volume 4, page 494—Samuel Simons release of mortgage to Tracey Freeman, "widow of the late Jacob," October 14, 1833.

Volume 4, pp. 319–20—Oliver and William Sherman to Tunis Green and Rosanna his wife—twenty-one rods of land with buildings bounded north by house lot of Harry Cooke, east by Main Street, south and west by Seth B. Jones, $500, September 23, 1834.

Volume 4, page 480—David Curtis to John Johnson—release of mortgage "with buildings thereon standing," September 5, 1833.

Volume 5, page 156—Mark Moore to Joseph Bloom and Isaac Hammond—lot and dwelling northwest corner Main and Whiting Streets, September 1, 1835 (deceased Hammond's interest conveyed to Joseph Bloom on March 13, 1843—Volume 9, page 740).

Volume 4, pp. 648–651—Philip Freeman remanded to jail for nonpayment of eighteen-dollar debt to Seth B. Jones, Susan Jones, & Caroline Hawley.

Volume 6, page 32—David Curtis to John Johnson—"small strip of land" (six rods) bounded east by Joel Freeman, $15, May 4, 1836.

Volume 6, page 54—conveyance by Isaac Whiting to John Tucker, June 14, 1836.

Volume 6, page 349—David Curtis to Lawson Sherman of Bridgeport—lot bounded north by Whiting Street, east by John Johnson, south by Pond Gutter, west by heirs of Aaron Hawley (deceased), $60, April 1, 1837.

Volume 6, page 350—David Curtis to Lawson Sherman—mortgage of above property, $60, April 1, 1837.

Volume 7, page 41—mortgage of above property "with buildings thereon standing," $40.

Volume 7, page 355—Lawson Sherman of Monroe to David Curtis—property "with the dwelling houses thereon standing including all the stone belonging to me on and near the premesis," $300, April 9, 1839.

(NOTE: Volume 2, page 650—lease by Ezra Gregory to Lawson Sherman for use as a carpenter's shop in 1827 makes it probable that he was a speculative builder—Sherman died in Monroe on January 8, 1842, at age forty-seven).

Volume 7, page 103—Isaac Burroughs to William Allen—lot on south side of Whiting Street between Broad and Main Streets, June 19, 1838.

Volume 7, page 431—Isaac Burroughs to John Gowdy—lot on south side of Whiting Street bounded east by William Allen, July 26, 1849.

Volume 8, page 233—Ezra Gregory to Simeon Dickson—property bounded east by Broad Street, north and west by grantor, south by Colored Episcopal Ebeneezer Church, $300, May 11, 1841.

Volume 8, page 253—David Curtis to William H. Davis of New York—thirteen rods of land with dwelling house bounded north by Whiting Street, east by Alson B. Judd, south and west by grantor, $300, June 28, 1841 (Volume 8, page 254—$100 mortgage; Volume 8, page 256—land between house lot and Pond Gutter, $25, July 17, 1841; Volume 8, page 542—$150 mortgage from Philo Hurd, November 2, 1841).

Volume 8, page 151—David Curtis to Alson B. Judd of Bridgeport—twelve rods land with dwelling house bounded north by Whiting Street, east by John Johnson, $300, January 28, 1841.

Volume 10, page 63—Ezra Gregory to Salisbury Lane of Bridgeport—south half of dwelling house bounded east by Broad Street, south by Zion Church, $162, November 4, 1843.

Volume 10, page 177—Ezra Gregory to Samuel Serrington of Bridgeport—north half of dwelling house bounded east by Broad Street, south by Salisbury Lane, March 30, 1844.

Volume 10, page 118—David Curtis to Minerva Simons of Bridgeport—twelve rods land with dwelling house bounded north by Whiting Street, west by William R. Davis, $140, January 18, 1844.

Volume 11, page 45—Josiah Fayerweather to Edward A. Jackson of New York—31½ rods of land bounded west by Broad Street, south by Whiting Street, north by Jane Sterling, east by Joseph Bloom, $220, August 15, 1845.

Volume 12, page 15—Ezra Gregory to Maria Hawley, wife of Grant A. Hawley—land on Gregory Street one hundred feet west of west line of church property.

Volume 12, page 19—Seth B. Jones to Rachel Simons of Southbury—land on Broad Street, $168, August 19, 1846.

Volume 12, page 22—Joseph Bloom mortgage to Nelson H. Judd, $160, August 19, 1846.

Volume 12, page 38—Sherwood Sterling to George W. Francis of Bridgeport—land bounded south by Joseph Bloom and Edward A. Jackson, west on Broad Street, north on William Johnson, east by Tunis Green, $100, September 11, 1846.

Volume 12, page 39—Sherwood Sterling to William Johnson of New York City—land bounded north by Harry Cook, east by Tunis Green, south by George W. Francis, west by Broad Street, September 11, 1846.

Volume 12, page 237—Seth B. Jones to Eliza Hayes (wife of Moses)—land bounded south by Whiting Street with dwelling house, $144 (see Bridgeport Probate Records, Volume 30, page 216).

Volume 13, page 137—Ezra Gregory to Harry Morris land bounded south by contemplated highway (Gregory Street), $105, September 29, 1845.

Volume 13, page 141—Ezra Gregory to William Allen—land bounded east by M.E. Society (colored), south by contemplated highway (Gregory Street), $105, September 29, 1845.

Volume 15, page 46—George Baldwin to William Allen "of Brooklyn, Long Island"—note secured by household goods (enumerated), May 28, 1850.

Volume 15, page 511—Quitclaim deed by Stephen Hawley to Grant and Maria Hawley—twenty-one rods of land "with buildings thereon standing," November 26, 1850.

Volume 17, page 604—Isaac Whiting loan to J. Emory Burr secured by household goods (enumerated).

Volume 19, page 678—Seth B. Jones to Presence Jackson—one-dollar lot bounded east on Main Street, south on Tunis Green and George W. Francis, west on Broad Street, north on heirs of Zalmon Hawley, December 1, 1853.

Volume 22, page 496—Thomas Burns and James Merritt—mechanics lien vs. Zion A.M.E. Church, "bounded west by the Misses Freeman," for work performed repairing building between September 10 and November 18, 1859, $217, January 7, 1860.

Volume 24, page 603—Tracey Loudon, William Freeman, Charles Freeman, Truman Freeman, and Mrs. Mary J. Pitts (heirs of Jacob and Tracey Freeman) to John & Zilpha Feeley—one-dollar south half of dwelling house, May 16, 1859.

(NOTE: Volume 10, page 708—property conveyed from the estate of Benjamin Freeman to Mark Moore, July 15, 1843; Volume 10, page 758—property conveyed from the estate of Benjamin's wife Dinah to Sherwood Sterling, January 20, 1844).

Volume 29, page 492—William Freeman of New Haven grants Power of Attorney to wife Mary C. Freeman of Bridgeport to sell land bounded east by Broad Street, "other sides by parties unknown," May 12, 1864.

Notes

Chapter 4

1. Stratford Land Records, vol. 33, p. 329.
2. *Ibid.*, vol. 33, p. 341.
3. Samuel Orcutt, *A History of the Old Town of Stratford and the City of Bridgeport* (Bridgeport: Fairfield County Historical Society, 1886) pp. 554, 719.
4. *Ibid.*
5. Stratford Land Records, vol. 33, pp. 428, 431.
6. *Bridgeport Standard*, September 29, 1862.
7. Orcutt, *History of Stratford and Bridgeport*, p. 664.
8. Bridgeport Land Records, vol. 1, p. 237.
9. Stratford Land Records, vol. 29, p. 415.
10. Bridgeport Land Records, vol. 3, p. 433.
11. *Ibid.*, vol. 4, pp. 648–651.
12. *Ibid.*, vol. 2, p. 6.
13. *Ibid.*, vol. 3, p. 328.
14. *Ibid.*, vol. 4, p. 43.
15. *Ibid.*, vol. 15, p. 558.
16. 1850 Bridgeport Census.
17. Bridgeport Land Records, vol. 3, p. 418.
18. Bridgeport Vital Records—Marriages, vol. 2, p. 131.
19. "Mary Freeman's Will," *Bridgeport Standard*, March 8, 1884, line 24.
20. See the lampblack/turpentine works discussed above; Bridgeport Land Records, vol. 3, p. 292.
21. *Ibid.*, p. 655.
22. Article on local news page, *Bridgeport Standard*, August 17, 1875.
23. Deed naming Joel Freeman as one of the heirs to the Turkey Hill Indians, General Assembly Papers, African Americans [sic], 1821–1869, State Archives Record Group No. 002, Box 32, Folder 8, Document 12, Connecticut State Library, Hartford, CT.

24. Vol. 32, pp. 10, 13.
25. *Ibid.*, vol. 24, p. 265.
26. Bridgeport Land Records, vol. 5, June 12, 1835, pp. 100, 101.
27. *Ibid.*, vol. 9, p. 734.
28. *Ibid.*, vol. 5, pp. 104, 432.
29. "Petition of Joel Freeman," General Assembly Papers, African Americans [sic], 1821–1869, State Archives Record Group No. 002, Box 1, Folder 16, Connecticut State Library, Hartford, CT.
30. Bridgeport Land Records, vol. 11, p. 395.
31. *Ibid.*, vol. 22, p.142.
32. Married 1824; Orange Vital Records, vol. 1, p. 2.
33. p. 234.
34. Death notice, *Bridgeport Standard*, May 5, 1865.
35. Bridgeport Land Records, vol. 22, p. 1311–12.
36. Excavated October 1885; paper describing findings printed in the Bridgeport *Daily Standard*, November 16, 1885.
37. pp. xxxix, xl.
38. pp. 21, 22.
39. Bridgeport Land Records, vol. 4, p. 33.
40. *Ibid.*, vol. 4, p. 178.
41. *Ibid.*, p. 179.
42. Place of birth shown on his daughter Ellen's 1902 death record.
43. Bridgeport Land records, vol. 19, p. 678.
44. *Ibid.*, vol. 39, p. 756.
45. *Ibid.*, vol. 4, p. 271.
46. *Ibid.*, p. 319.
47. Redding Vital Records, vol. 1, p. 114.
48. Bridgeport Vital Records—Deaths, vol. 1, March 16, 1856, p. 7.
49. Death notice, *Bridgeport Standard*, July 21, 1883.
50. Newtown Vital Records, vol. 3, p. 75.
51. Bridgeport Land Records, vol. 9, p. 318.
52. *Ibid.*, volume 8, p. 232; vol. 9, p. 298.
53. Bridgeport Probate Records, vol. 14, p. 468.
54. Described as a resident of Stratford in 1858; Bridgeport Land Records, vol. 22, p. 317.
55. *Ibid.*, vol. 5, p. 156.
56. Bridgeport Vital Records—Deaths, vol. 2, p. 52.
57. *Ibid.*,—Marriages, vol. 1, p. 10.
58. *Ibid.*, vol. 1, p. 3.
59. Bridgeport Land Records, vol. 9, p. 740.
60. *Ibid.*, vol. 12, p. 22.
61. Southbury Vital Records, vol. 3, p. 117.
62. Conversation between Walters Memorial historian Mary L. McDuffie and octogenarian descendant Emma Stewart, 8/10/03.

63. 1855 *City Directory*.
64. Bridgeport Vital Records—Marriages, vol. 1, p. 85.
65. 1870–71 *City Directory*.
66. Bridgeport Land Records, vol. 60, p. 721.
67. Name changed to A.M.E. in 1850; State Archives Record Group 002, Box 1, Folder 20, Connecticut State Library.

Chapter 5

68. Bridgeport Land Records, vol. 7, pp. 859, 860.
69. Orcutt, *History of Stratford and Bridgeport*, p. 853.
70. Bridgeport Land Records, vol. 11, p. 64.
71. Bridgeport Vital Records, vol. 1, p. 70.
72. *Ibid.*, vol. 1, p. 65.
73. 1880–81 *City Directory*.
74. Bridgeport Vital Records—Marriages, vol. 3, p. 142.
75. See page 68.
76. Stratford Land Records, vol. 35, p. 610.
77. *Republican Farmer*, April 5, 1837.
78. Preserved in the collections of the Connecticut Historical Society.
79. Stratford Land Records, vol. 36, p. 284.
80. *Ibid.*, vol. 36, p. 438.
81. *Ibid.*, vol. 37, p. 2.
82. *Ibid.*, vol. 37, pp. 10, 12.
83. *Bridgeport Standard*, October 7, 1876.

Chapter 6

84. Bridgeport Land Records, vol. 6, pp. 349, 350.
85. *Ibid.*, vol. 7, p. 355.
86. *Ibid.*, vol. 8, p. 151.
87. Newtown Vital Records, vol. 3, p. 30.
88. 1830 Danbury Census.
89. *Bridgeport Republican Standard*, August 18, 1846.
90. Bridgeport Land Records, vol. 8, p. 253.
91. Marriage notice, *Spirit of the Times*, March 21, 1832; *Bridgeport Messenger*, March 28, 1832.
92. *Bridgeport Republican Standard*, October 17, 1848.
93. Bridgeport Land Records, vol. 10, p. 118.
94. Southbury Vital Records, vol. 1, p. 149.
95. Bridgeport Land Records, vol. 12, p. 19.
96. Obituaries, *Bridgeport Standard*, December 24 and 26, 1891.
97. 1870 Bridgeport Census.
98. Bridgeport Land Records, vol. 11, p. 395.

99. His reminiscences are contained in an article in the *Bridgeport Sunday Post*, December 17, 1911.
100. Bridgeport Land Records, vol. 7, p. 103.
101. Bridgeport Vital Records—Marriages, vol. 1, p. 100.
102. "Main Street, Concluded" from Julian H. Sterling Scrapbook, collected newspaper columns, "Do You Remember?" series, Historical Collections, Bridgeport Public Library, Bridgeport, CT.
103. Bridgeport Land Records, vol. 7, p. 431.
104. *Ibid.*, vol. 8, p. 233.
105. Bridgeport Vital Records—Marriages, vol. 1, October 17, 1841, p. 45.
106. Bridgeport Land Records, vol. 26, p. 285.
107. See pp. 58-60.
108. Monroe Vital Records, vol. 1, p. 51.
109. Bridgeport Land Records, vol. 10, p. 63.
110. *Ibid.*, vol. 10, p. 177.
111. *Ibid.*, vol. 11, p. 45.
112. *Ibid.*, vol. 12, pp. 38, 39.
113. *Ibid.*, vol. 8, p. 606.
114. *Ibid.*, vol. 13, p. 141.
115. *Ibid.*, vol. 13, p. 137.
116. *Ibid.*, vol. 15, p. 511.
117. Bridgeport Vital Records—Marriages, vol. 1, p. 55.
118. Bridgeport Land Records, vol. 17, p. 349.

Chapter 7

119. Bridgeport Land Records, vol. 13, pp. 137, 141.
120. Bridgeport Vital Records—Marriages, Philander Pitts to Antoinette Gibson on January 10, 1834, vol. 1, p. 21.
121. Bridgeport Land Records, vol. 22, p. 208.
122. p. 117.
123. Born in Pennsylvania, 1810.
124. Born in Delaware, 1810, with her parents born in Jamaica, West Indies.
125. Bridgeport Land Records, vol. 30, p. 216.
126. Stratford Land Records, vol. 37, p. 10.
127. Obituary, *Bridgeport Standard*, July 21, 1883.
128. Derby Land Records, vol. 32, p. 10.
129. *Ibid.*, vol. 32, p. 13.
130. *Bridgeport Standard*, March 8, 1884.
131. Derby Land Records, vol. 35, p. 148.
132. Bridgeport Land Records, vol. 13, p. 254.
133. *Ibid.*, vol. 14, p. 97.
134. *Ibid.*, p. 98.

135. New Haven Vital Records—Marriages, William Freeman of Derby on November 21, 1841, vol. 6, p. 30.
136. Thought to be the mother of James.
137. Bridgeport Probate Records, vol. 18, p. 471.
138. Bridgeport Land Records, vol. 40, p. 102.
139. Bridgeport Probate Records, vol. 32, pp. 142–143.
140. See *Commemorative Biographical Record of Fairfield County* (1899), p. 206.
141. See articles in *Bridgeport Standard*, May 5 and May 9, 1891.
142. Bridgeport Land Records, vol. 81, pp. 478–80.
143. *Ibid.*, vol. 81, p. 669.
144. *Ibid.*, vol. 82, pp. 188, 552.
145. October 24, 1882.
146. July 14, 1884.
147. Bridgeport Land Records, vol. 18, p. 114.
148. *Ibid.*, vol. 11, p. 64.
149. Orcutt, *History of Stratford and Bridgeport*, p. 638.
150. "Cloud to be Removed," *Bridgeport Standard*, November 4, 1887.
151. Listed in the 1850 Census for New York City as a fifty-year-old mulatto undertaker, born in Virginia.
152. Bridgeport Land Records, vol. 7, p. 632.
153. *Ibid.*, vol. 12, p. 648.
154. Portion of today's West Broadway between Canal and West 4th Streets.
155. Bridgeport Land Records, vol. 18, pp. 607, 613.
156. *Ibid.*, vol. 18, p. 739.
157. *Ibid.*, vol. 18, p. 763.
158. *Ibid.* vol. 21, p. 195.

Chapter 8

159. Served 1836–1849.
160. Obituary, *Bridgeport Evening Post*, September 26, 1894, p. 1.
161. "Journal of William Sherman," January 5, 1875.
162. Fairfield Land Records, vol. 57, p. 247.
163. Papers of Richard Ambler, Connecticut Historical Society Archives, Hartford, CT.
164. Obituary, *Bridgeport Standard*, September 14, 1891.
165. Died April 21, 1896, age seventy-nine.

Chapter 9

166. Died March 10, 1862, age seventy-two; Stratford Vital Records, vol. A, p. 67.
167. Vol. C, p. 518.
168. *Bridgeport Standard*, June 13, 1888.
169. Vol. 53, pp. 512, 513.
170. Stratford Vital Records, vol. A, p. 67.

171. *Ibid.*, vol. A, p. 65.
172. Journal entry dated August 29, 1875.
173. Died December 23, 1892, age sixty-three.
174. Stratford Land Records, vol. 53, p. 514.
175. Stratford Vital Records—Deaths, vol. B, pp. 88, 94.

Chapter 10

176. Bridgeport Land Records, vol. 29, p. 328.
177. *Ibid.*, vol. 38, p. 54.
178. *Ibid.*, vol. 30, p. 812.
179. Orcutt, vol. 2, p. 906.
180. May 18, 1863.
181. Enrolled in the National Register of Historic Places as the William D. Bishop Cottage Development.
182. Anne Whelan, "The Park Becomes a Student Haven," *Bridgeport Sunday Post*, December 7, 1947.
183. p. 119.
184. *Bridgeport Daily Standard*, August 5, 1873.
185. Son of Harry and Mary Morris, discussed previously.
186. Conversation with Mary L. McDuffie, 8/25/03; the diary is presently in the possession of New York relatives and was not immediately available.
187. Orcutt, *History of Stratford and Bridgeport*, p. 818.
188. Bridgeport Vital Records—Marriages, vol. 1, p. 290.

Chapter 11

189. December 9, 1875.
190. Trumbull Land Records, vol. 11, p. 323.
191. *Ibid.*, p. 324.
192. *Ibid.*, vol. 12, p. 659.

Chapter 12

193. See *Bridgeport Tri-Weekly Standard*, September 5, 1853.
194. See article "Bridgeport Indians," *Bridgeport Standard*, November 30, 1886.
195. Bridgeport Land Records, vol. 862, p. 533; vol. 1132, p. 388.
196. Zion was renamed Walters Memorial early in the twentieth century for Bishop Alexander Walters, a former pastor.
197. Conversation on March 25, 2003.

Chapter 13

198. Vol. C, pp. 490, 491.
199. In 1850 he shared a double house with Charles and Susan Jackson, Presence's son and daughter-in-law; he married Caroline Jackson in 1850, and his daughter Olive married Hamilton Jackson at some point prior to 1860.

200. His partner in the ship's carpentry business, Reuben Cam, had married a Freeman from Orange.
201. It should also be noted that Pitts's second wife was Mary Ann Freeman, daughter of Jacob.
202. e.g. Antoinette and Henrietta Simonds.
203. Jane had a brother, Henry W., whose wife Julia gave birth to a daughter, Sarah, early in 1886—when this child died on January 4, 1887, her Bridgeport death record indicated she had been born on the Trumbull reservation.
204. Bridgeport Land Records, vol. 39, April 1, 1873, p. 756.

Chapter 14

205. p. 212.
206. *New Haven Register*, April 3, 1993.
207. *Bridgeport Post*, February 27, 1974.
208. February 28, 1974.
209. March 7, 1974.
210. Prior to this, incredible as it may seem, they were legally considered aliens.
211. October 17, 1976.
212. September 1, 2002.

Bibliography

Published Sources

Caulkins, Frances Manwaring. *History of Norwich, Connecticut.* Published by the author, 1866.

Commemorative Biographical Record of Fairfield County, Connecticut. Chicago: J.H. Beers & Co., 1899.

DeForest, John William. *History of the Indians of Connecticut.* Hartford: W.J. Hammersley, 1851.

Hurd, D. Hamilton. *A History of Fairfield County, Connecticut.* Philadelphia: J.W. Lewis & Co., 1881.

Menta, John P. *The Quinnipiac: Cultural Conflict in Southern New England.* New Haven: Yale University Publications in Anthropology, 2003.

Orcutt, Samuel. *A History of the Old Town of Derby 1642-1880.* Springfield, MA: Springfield Printing Co., 1880

———. *A History of the Old Town of Stratford and the City of Bridgeport.* Bridgeport: Fairfield County Historical Society, 1886.

Sterling, Julian H. *Space.* Bridgeport: Marigold-Foster Printing Co., 1904.

White, Alain C. *History of the Town of Litchfield 1720-1920.* Litchfield, CT: Litchfield Historical Society, 1920.

Periodicals

Batchelor, C.S., and R. Edward Steck. "Indian Archeology in and around Bridgeport, Connecticut." *Bulletin of the Archeological Society of Connecticut*, no. 12 (May, 1941).

Unpublished Manuscripts

"Letters of Edwards Johnson," Connecticut Historical Society Archives, Hartford, CT.

"Journal of William Sherman," in possession of Golden Hill Paugussett tribe.

"Papers of Richard Ambler,"Connecticut Historical Society Archives, Hartford, CT.

Church Records

Records of Bethel A.M.E. Church, Bridgeport, CT.
Records of Clinton A.M.E. Zion Church, Ansonia, CT.
Records of Golden Hill United Methodist Church, Bridgeport, CT.
Records of St. John's Episcopal Church, Bridgeport, CT.
Records of Walters Memorial A.M.E. Zion Church, Bridgeport, CT.

United States Census

Fairfield and New Haven Counties, Connecticut: 1810, 1820, 1830, 1840, 1850, 1860, 1870, 1880.
New York County, New York: 1850.

Land Records

City of Bridgeport
City of Derby
Town of Fairfield
Town of Monroe
Town of Stratford
Town of Trumbull

Probate Records

City of Bridgeport
Town of Huntington (became City of Shelton 1919)

Vital Records

City of Ansonia
City of Bridgeport
City of New Haven
Town of Newtown
Town of Orange
Town of Redding
Town of Southbury
Town of Stratford
Town of Trumbull

Other Materials

Bridgeport *City Directories*, 1855–1945.
Bridgeport newspapers on microfilm. Bridgeport Public Library.
General Assembly Papers. African Americans, 1821–1869. State Archives Record Group No. 002, Box 1, Folders 16 and 20. Connecticut State Library, Hartford, CT.
Hale Collection of Cemetery Headstone Inscriptions. Connecticut State Library, Hartford, CT.

Julian H. Sterling Scrapbook. Collected newspaper columns, "Do You Remember?" series. Historical Collections Bridgeport Public Library, Bridgeport, CT.
News clipping file. Historical Collections, Bridgeport Public Library.